KERYGMA AND COUNSELING

D0368352

HARPER'S MINISTERS PAPERBACK LIBRARY

KERYGMA AND COUNSELING

TOWARD A COVENANT ONTOLOGY
FOR SECULAR PSYCHOTHERAPY

by

Thomas C. Oden

Published in San Francisco by
HARPER & ROW, PUBLISHERS
New York, Hagerstown, San Francisco, London

First Harper & Row paperback edition published in 1978.

Hardcover edition originally published by The Westminster Press in 1966.

Scripture quotations from the Revised Standard Version of the Bible are used by permission.

KERYGMA AND COUNSELING. Copyright © 1966, 1978 by Thomas C. Oden. All rights reserved. Printed in the United States of America. No part of this book may be used or reproduced in any manner whatsoever without written permission except in the case of brief quotations embodied in critical articles and reviews. For information address Harper & Row, Publishers, Inc., 10 East 53rd Street, New York, N.Y. 10022. Published simultaneously in Canada by Fitzhenry & Whiteside Limited, Toronto.

BV4012
.O27
1978x

0 03928222

ISBN: 0-06-066346-4

LIBRARY OF CONGRESS CATALOG CARD NUMBER: 66-11516

The text of this book is printed on 100% recycled paper.

78 79 80 81 82 10 9 8 7 6 5 4 3 2 1

To
DR. ROBERT E. ELLIOTT, PERKINS SCHOOL OF THEOLOGY
DR. DON S. BROWNING, UNIVERSITY OF CHICAGO
DIVINITY SCHOOL
AND
DR. CHARLES H. MAHONE, COUNSELING CENTER,
TEXAS TECH.

GIFTED AND VALUED PARTNERS IN DIALOGUE
IN THEOLOGY AND PSYCHOTHERAPY.

CONTENTS

PREFACE TO THE PAPERBACK EDITION

The first edition of *Kerygma and Counseling* appeared in 1966, received more than its share of critical attention, and, according to most accounts, an appreciative readership. It soon became unavailable, however, and like many theological books of the 1960s was not reprinted. Meanwhile theology was on a trip of its own, going through an agonizing series of pseudochapters, media events, false starts, and identity confusions.

During this time *Kerygma and Counseling* continued to have a life of its own, passing through several phases of *sub rosa* editions. Now, twelve years later, it is a great pleasure to have it included in the Harper Ministers Paperback Library, where it can address a new generation of pastors and theological students still hungry for an appropriate integration of the best resources of theology and psychotherapy.

I am amused and delighted by the prospect that a theological position developed in the early 1960s might have fresh relevance for a new set of readers in the post-"revolutionary" present. I put revolutionary in ironic quotes because the promised theological revolutions of the messianic late 1960s and early 1970s have, by and large, misunderstood the perniciousness of sin, overestimated human potential, idealized autonomous individual freedom, and have in the meantime tended to become patricidal toward the Christian traditon. There remains a comic element in the awareness that a theological book might surprisingly be more suited to another audience than the one for which it was at first modestly and earnestly written.

Developments in the intervening years have left me strongly reassured on two points about which I was not fully certain in 1966: .

1. The therapeutic triad (accurate empathy, nonpossessive warmth, and congruence) upon which my argument hinges has received much wider confirmation and solid research support since 1966 from therapists of orientations other than that of Carl Rogers. (For a trackdown of these research reports, see my articles in the *Journal of Humanistic Psychology:* "A Populist's View of Psychotherapeutic Deprofessionalization," 14:2, Spring, 1974, and "Consumer Interests in Therapeutic Outcome Studies," 15:3, Summer, 1975.) The overall effect of this detailed research is to show that no therapy, Rogerian or otherwise, can function optimally without empathy, unconditional positive regard, and authenticity. So it should not be assumed that the triadic theoretical orientation that I utilized in 1966 is so heavily indebted to client-centered therapy that it cannot be related to other orientations. In fact to those who have perceived my argument as too deeply dependent upon Rogers, I would only remind them to take seriously my own sober criticisms of Rogers at the end of Chapter III.

2. While many in the late 1960s thought Karl Barth to be a sinking dogmatic ship to be abandoned posthaste, I was convinced that his analogical method offered rich new possibilities (although he was not fully aware of them) for the deteriorating dialogue with psychotherapy. Since then it has become increasingly apparent that, however much we may disagree with Barth, we must take him seriously

as the preeminent Protestant theologian of this century, and acknowledge that his analogical method has wide applicability far beyond its original conception. Although Barth's work has not developed in America into a stuffy scholasticism as it did in Europe, I am happy to note that many of the Barthian themes that were being prematurely abandoned in the late sixties (the intrinsic relation between judgment and grace, the authority of the Word, the ethics of responsible freedom, and a thoroughgoing Christological humanism) have by the late seventies come back to the fore.

When as a young instructor I first began the adventure that this book represents, its basic thesis (the juxtaposition of Carl Rogers and Karl Barth) was so outrageous that at times I myself wondered if the whole idea was merely a flight of fancy. During the past twelve years, however, I have been generously reassured by many pastors and counselors not only that these analogical ideas have an immanent plausibility that corresponds with their experience, but also that they have applicability and usefulness for their functioning as counselors in the Christian tradition.

So the germinative insight of *Kerygma and Counseling* — the linking of a therapy of human self-disclosure with a theology of divine self-disclosure — seems to me to be at least as viable now, and possibly more so, than when first offered. I have chosen to keep the original text and suppress my temptation to tamper with it and update it, a process that itself would soon be out of date if I were attempting an up-to-the-minute report.

If I were writing the book today as if it had never been written, doubtless I would write it somewhat differently, partly because I am a somewhat changed person with shifted interests and passions — now more middle-aged, a bit stodgier and more traditional. If I were writing it now

I would be more congenial and less defensive toward the "specifically religious approaches to therapy" that were excoriated several times in the first chapter (pp. 19, 26-27, 30). Some of the movements that were touted as "emerging" in 1966 (such as lay theological renewal and demythologization) are obviously not any longer emerging, whereas some influences that I thought at the time to be receding (pragmatic Protestant liberalism) have shown themselves to be amazingly resilient and tenacious. I would now place more stress upon the points made in the section "A Stern Word on Worldly Dialogue" if I were writing the book today. I would also try harder to correct the misreading of the text as expounding "cheap grace" or uncritical universalism. I have attempted to clarify this point in a series of lectures at the School of Psychology of Fuller Theological Seminary (see *After Therapy What?*, edited by Neil C. Warren, Springfield: Charles C. Thomas, 1974). In fact, many of the points of criticism raised by reviewers of this book in the 1960s have been addressed in that lecture series, and especially in the last chapter, a "Response" to my symposium partners and other critics. So I will not at this point attempt any further dialogue with my critics, except to acknowledge how valuable their criticisms have been to me in my subsequent writings.

The sequel volume spoken of in the first footnote to this book did appear as *Contemporary Theology and Psychotherapy*, (Philadelphia: Westminster, 1967), followed successively by five other volumes in the same general subject area of the dialogue between theology and therapy: *The Structure of Awareness* (Nashville: Abingdon, 1969), *The Intensive Group Experience: The New Pietism* (Philadelphia: Westminster, 1972), *Game Free: The Meaning of Intimacy* (New York: Harper & Row, 1974), *After Therapy What?*, and *TAG: The Transactional Awareness Game*

(New York: Harper & Row, 1976). *Kerygma and Counseling* was the first and the pacesetter for this series, and to my mind an essential propaedeutic for all that followed. Although it is too much to ask of the reader, I would sincerely hope that this text of 1966 would be read and viewed in the light of the problems further discussed in my subsequent writings of the same genre, which in various ways sharpen, amend, and amplify the thesis of this book.

T.C.O.

Drew University
Madison, N.J.
Epiphany, 1978

PREFACE TO THE FIRST EDITION

The central thesis of this inquiry is that *there is an implicit assumption hidden in all effective psychotherapy which is made explicit in the Christian proclamation.* Our project focuses upon an exploration of the relation between a psychotherapy of human self-disclosure and a theology of God's self-disclosure.

If this essay is addressed to the pastor who has become uneasily aware that there is something inconsistent between the content of his preaching and the form of his counseling relationships, it is equally addressed to the practicing psychotherapist who yearns for some sort of theological undergirding for his daily work and longs for the church to speak clearly and meaningfully of God's action in the midst of his human — all too human — action.

In his preface to *On Becoming a Person,* Carl Rogers speaks of his "search for a suitable audience" for what he has to say. One significant audience with which Rogers has never gained a hearing is an influential group of kerygmatic theologians, or theologians of revelation, who are concerned to begin their theological discussion exclusively with the assumption that God has disclosed himself in history in a way that necessarily calls for a radical reformulation of the human question. Whatever one might think of this theological stance, it can be persuasively argued that these theologians constitute the main current of Protestant theology in our time, with such divergent schools as those of Bultmann, Bonhoeffer, and Barth all agreeing on the basic axiom of the necessity of revelation for all authentic speech about God. Although Carl Rogers has certainly had a long-term rapport and lively dialogue with the disappearing generation of pragmatic American Protestant liberalism, his conversation with postliberal theology has been utterly abortive and disappointing. If Rogers himself has done little to encourage this dialogue, it has also been sadly neglected by kerygmatic theologians who have written off Rogers as a " cockeyed optimist " with no serious conception of the radical fallenness of man and with no real promise for dialogue with a seriously confessional, Christological, Biblical theology. There is a sense in which my whole effort is an attempt to show the hidden similarities, despite basic differences, between a Barthian theology of divine self-disclosure and a Rogerian therapy of human self-disclosure. Like Rogers', however, our discussion will undoubtedly be a book in search of an audience. Hopefully the dialogue will be carried on not only by parish ministers and professional religionists, but also and more so by clinicians and therapists who are beginning to awaken to the implications of the emerging lay theological renewal of our time, and who wish to relate their therapeutic self-understanding to contemporary existentialist and ecumenical theology.

Although I cannot agree wholeheartedly with the direction that undoubtedly has been set for Protestant pastoral care by its three most influential contemporary spokesmen, Paul Tillich, Eduard Thurneysen, and Seward Hiltner, I would be amiss if I failed to acknowledge my deep indebtedness to these three distinguished theologians with whom my thinking has been in constant interaction during the entire period of my reflection upon this issue. In a subsequent volume now in preparation during this current sabbatical year at Heidelberg, I will attempt to spell out my own responses to the major contributions each of them has made to recent Protestant pastoral theology.[1] Especially to Seward Hiltner do I wish to express a word of personal thanks for the detailed and helpful criticism that he gave to this entire manuscript. Unfortunately, the theologians who have most deeply shaped my own thinking on these issues (Teilhard de Chardin, H. R. Niebuhr, Barth, Bultmann, and Bonhoeffer) have had pitifully little to say about psychotherapy as such.

The nurturing of this proposal has proceeded on the basis of a deep theological intuition which I simply could not deny but felt compelled to clarify for myself. My first attempt at a written clarification of this persistent hunch was in an essay first read in 1960 for the Phillips faculty colloquium, later published in *Continuum* (Summer, 1964) as "Revelation in Psychotherapy I" (with a rejoinder by Fr. Godin, of Belgium). A similar statement, but couched in the language of the psychotherapeutic community, appeared in the *Journal of Individual Psychology* (1964, 20, 69-78, used by permission), entitled "A Theologian's View of the Process of Psychotherapy," which first put me in touch with a number of European therapists with whom I am now in conversation. I am grateful to editor Heinz Ansbacher who took the risk of publishing that statement from the viewpoint of a theology of revelation in a clinically oriented journal.

The later stage of the development of this manuscript has emerged in continuous creative dialogue with Dr. Don S. Browning, now of Chicago Divinity School, whose forthcoming book *Atonement and Psychotherapy* will bear evidence of our interaction on the question of analogy. Although we move in visibly different directions on such crucial issues as theological method and Christology, we have shared in a deeply meaningful conversation over the past two years, leading both of us to wonder what strange sort of providence could have brought us together for those two fruitful years in the remote spot of Enid, Oklahoma, with our uniquely similar concerns for developing a Protestant understanding of psychotherapy on the basis of a revised doctrine of analogy. Don Browning, more than anyone else, has pointed me toward the potential *rapprochement* between Hartshorne's process analogies and the *analogia fidei*.

To my former teachers, Albert C. Outler, who first framed for me the penetrating issue of the relation of therapy and theology, and Robert E. Elliott, who first introduced me to the views of Carl Rogers, I owe a continuing word of thanks. To Dr. Sidney Jourard, Dr. Frank M. Bockus, and to my colleague at Phillips Seminary, Dr. Fred Craddock, I am indebted for providing special assistance with the manuscript.

Especially to Dr. Carl R. Rogers I am deeply grateful not only for providing me with much of the impetus and inspiration that motivated me to do work in psychotherapy but also for reviewing portions of this manuscript and reassuring me that, despite differences in viewpoint, " I did not come across any instance in which I felt you had seriously misunderstood me." [2] Finally, I am sincerely grateful to the Danforth Foundation and the Society for Religion in Higher Education for the grant that has enabled my current study of existential psychotherapy and *Daseinsanalyse* in the department of psychiatry at Heidelberg.

Keenly aware that this proposal is presented in a rapidly changing historical situation, and that it intends to speak to a special audience at a particular nexus of history in which there are constantly shifting modulations and mutations in our understanding of therapy which will undoubtedly soon outmode the thesis itself and hopefully improve upon it, I think we would do well to confess from the outset the radically contingent, historically relative character of all constructive thinking today. It surely should not take very long for someone to come up with a much more adequate statement of the deeper intention of this thesis than I have articulated. In fact, it still astonishes me that someone has not already done so, since the core of the proposal is so simple, since Barth's *analogia fidei* has now been available as a staple theological construct for some thirty years, and since Rogers' work has been in its mature stage for almost two decades. But we can only hope that some readers in this volatile, changing modern situation will find it currently meaningful or useful, with little illusion or anticipation that this modest discussion will be valid for more than a decade or two, due to the fast-moving pace of studies in psychotherapy and theology.

T. C. O.

Heidelberg, Germany

CHAPTER I

THE IMPLICIT ASSUMPTION
OF EFFECTIVE PSYCHOTHERAPY

Our question is: In what sense is the psychotherapeutic process analogous to the self-disclosure of God? The basic issue may be variously framed: How is a psychotherapy of *human self-disclosure* related to a theology of *divine self-disclosure?* How does the kerygma illuminate the counseling process?

Among numerous efforts of the past generation to clarify the relation between psychotherapy and theology, many ponderous attempts have been made to formulate the relationship in terms of an analogy. The few successes that have been achieved have usually paid the price of a regrettable dilution of the Christian understanding of revelation.

It is to the interest of both therapist and theologian to distinguish sharply between the psychotherapeutic process and revelation, however much they may be shown to be in certain ways analogous. The serious psychotherapist makes no extravagant claims about his work as somehow equivalent to divine salvation, nor is the discriminating theologian interested in trying to equate psychological adjustment with God's justification of man in Jesus Christ. The responsible theologian no more wants to take counseling captive to religious categories than the therapist wants to circumscribe the deity with psychoanalysis.

The growing edge of this dialogue must not be simply the further elaboration of the ways in which therapeutic experience is like religious experience,[1] nor merely the attempt to understand one another in our differences, although this must continue. If the current dialogue is to emerge as something more than a repetition of past inadequacies, it must now turn toward a fresh, new form of analogy, viz., the *analogia fidei*, faith's analogy between the activity of God and the ontological presuppositions of the counselor.[2] Together we must inquire into what the therapist quietly assumes about the nature of being as he goes about his task, and how that assumption corresponds with the principal concern of theology.

The whole concept of analogy has undergone intensive reexamination with the work of Karl Barth, who rejects the traditional notion of analogy in favor of an analogy of faith (*analogia fidei*). The traditional use of analogy, the *analogia entis* (analogy of being) of natural theology, begins with a natural entity or relationship (e.g., the psychotherapeutic interview) and then searches for some attribute of God with which it corresponds (e.g., the healing activity of God). *Analogia fidei* instead begins with the divine word or activity as it is received and understood in faith and perceives the natural entity or relationship from the vantage point of the divine activity (e.g., first we come to know of the healing action of God in the Christ event; then, having learned the character of authentic healing, we may perceive psychotherapeutic healing as analogous to the healing action of God). *Analogia fidei* turns the natural analogy around, reading from the Christ event to human events, from God's gracious action to human action, from God's interpretation of man to human interpretation, understanding human words under the illuminating power of the divine word.[3]

The proposal that we shall pursue is that the *psychotherapeutic process, although distinct from revelation, implicitly presupposes an ontological assumption* — Deus pro nobis — *which is made explicit in the Christian kerygma and clarified in faith's response to revelation, and it is therefore possible by means of the analogy of faith to perceive Christologically the so-called secular counseling situation as the arena of God's self-disclosure.*

Several *working definitions* may assist the reader in following this argument: In our usage, *kerygma* means proclamation, or announcement of good news. *Christian kerygma* means the preaching or announcement of the good news that Jesus is the Christ. *Christ* means expected deliverer, the fulfillment of human hopes. *Theology* is a deliberate attempt at a self-consistent ordering of our human self-understanding in response to the Christian kerygma. *Counseling* is a process of conversation with a congruent human brother who mediates empathetic understanding and unconditional positive regard with a view toward resolving destructive inner conflicts. *Psychotherapy* is a depth mode of counseling with a trained professional who is presumably capable of helping troubled persons to resolve inner conflicts.[4] *Effective* psychotherapy or counseling occurs when the conversational process achieves its goal of congruence, openness to experience, personal self-disclosure and self-understanding. *Accepting reality* refers to the source of self-affirmation in psychotherapy that is mediated through the counselor, and, according to the Christian kerygma, made known in history in the Christ event.

1. Sharpening the Question

To most therapists who are even vaguely familiar with the name of Karl Barth, it might seem ludicrous to juxtapose his views with the views of Carl Rogers. Likewise,

to postliberal theologians who are roughly familiar with
the work of Carl Rogers, nothing seems more obtuse than
to suggest that Rogers' work parallels Barth's Christological doctrine of man and revelation. No one to my knowledge has been more consistent than Rogers in asserting
that the self must tap resources within itself if it is to
function fully.[5] No one has been more consistent than
Barth in asserting that in Jesus Christ man finds his true
humanity.[6] They seem to live in two different and irre-
concilable communities of discourse. Nevertheless, it is
a major concern of this discussion to inquire whether
these two views, which find their chief representatives in
Barth and Rogers, are capable of joining dialogue, and if
so, what sort of conclusions might result. *Can a humanistic therapy and a theology of revelation be meaningfully
and self-consistently conjoined in a single ministry of
preaching and counseling?* [7]

Far from being an abstract question, this perplexity is
more and more beginning to be experienced as a serious
existential dilemma by ministers and teachers who have
been nurtured in a theology of revelation, but who are
simultaneously convinced that client-centered counseling
is the best help they can offer, and are convinced that
some special " religious " approach to couseling is less
effective. I, myself, as a teacher of theology and pastoral
care, have been forced to grapple with this question almost daily. In my classes in theology I have found myself
being more and more committed to a demythologized
form of the classical Protestant understanding of the radical fallenness of man, alienated from authentic life, in
bondage to a false understanding of existence in such a
great degree that he is blind to his own predicament of
blindness, unaware of his estrangement and of the gift of
God's grace in Jesus Christ which provides a new possi-

bility for an appropriate self-understanding. In my classes in pastoral care, however, and in counseling students, I find myself just as deeply committed to the assumptions of client-centered therapy, which rely exclusively on the resources for renewal already within the self.[8] For a number of years, I have had a strong intuition that these two approaches, ostensibly so different, had some kind of hidden affinity, and that one ministry could self-consistently embody them both. I have looked in vain for someone to spell out for me how they are related. If therapists have failed to take seriously revelation, theologians have also failed to account for the hidden kerygmatic center of the process of therapy. But if both perspectives can be internalized, how are they interrelated?

We must begin by rejecting that position which would make special claims for a " Christian therapy," or an understanding of counseling which would be determinatively informed by faith.[9] The clinical evidence seems all too clear that a disbelieving therapist can be quite as effective in providing the individual with the possibility of genuine self-awareness and openness to experience as can one who is self-consciously Christian.

The good news of God, to which preaching is a witness, announces the gift of divine forgiving love which calls man to a new understanding of himself. Therapy is not proclamation. Insofar as it seeks to impose upon the individual an " answer " that is not his own answer, it already operates outside the frame of reference of his private world, and therefore usually proves ineffective.[10] The task of the therapist is not advising or moralizing but clarification in a setting of acceptance.

He who seriously takes upon himself the task of proclaiming the Christian gospel, however, must be willing to stand in a judgmental relation to his hearer, since the gospel stands in judgment of all false understanding. Yet he who seriously takes upon himself the task of counseling must be willing to deny himself all judgmental attitudes toward the troubled individual, since the central purpose of therapy is the discovery of a relationship in which the individual is unthreatened by outsiders' judgments and is free to explore his feelings and share them for self-clarification.[11]

The Christian community acts on the assumption that God has spoken to man in Jesus Christ. It cannot apologize for this presupposition, but instead must ceaselessly witness to it as the ground of an appropriate self-understanding. Effective therapy does not necessarily share this assumption (although it may). It does not depend upon any explicit witness to God's action. It is a healing art whose end is clearer insight into one's personal and interpersonal history. But what assumptions are presupposed in this process?

The question that we are today pressed to ask ourselves is: *How can a therapy which assumes that man has within himself the capacity for appropriate self-direction (provided he has a safe context in which to explore his feelings) be consistent with a theology which assumes that the possibility for authentic existence comes to man as a gift mediated once for all through the self-disclosure of God in Jesus Christ?*

2. The Ontology of Acceptance

We are at least safe in observing that most of the categories of classical theology are recapitulated in an analogous fashion in the therapeutic experience. Guilt, idolatry, forgiveness, sanctification, faith, love — all these and many more theological concepts have their counterpart in therapy. This is nothing new, and has been talked about by many theologians and a few therapists for over a generation. It is clear to both sides that the analogy is present. It would not be incorrect to say that hundreds of attempts have been made to articulate the nature of this *rapprochement*. The chief difficulty that the discriminating theologian has with most of these attempts is their readiness to abandon, hide, weaken, neglect, or allegorize the revelation of God in Jesus Christ, the divine self-disclosure that is not only the basis for all Christian theology but the *raison d'être* of the Christian community. The *rapprochement* of theology and therapy must not be based upon the capitulation of theology to the limited language and world view of nineteenth-century science, nor upon a misunderstanding of the function of the therapist.

When we are honest with ourselves as Protestant pastors and counselors, we often find ourselves involved in an inconsistency. We preach on the assumption that salvation is a gift of God and we counsel on the assumption that salvation is a type of Socratic achievement of insight. These seem frankly and utterly inconsistent. The proposal we would like to offer as a possible solution to this dilemma is as follows: *There is a tacit ontological assumption of all effective therapy not that it is merely the counselor who accepts the client but that the client is acceptable as a human being by the ground of being itself, and that the final reality that we confront in life is for us —* Deus pro nobis. To clarify and support this assertion is now our task.

Since all human action is based on some self-understanding involving implicit metaphysical, ontological, and cosmological assumptions regardless of how inarticulate or inaccurate that self-understanding might be, we can say that all human action has philosophical and theological presuppositions. It is the task of philosophy and theology to inquire into the adequacy of these presuppositions. The action of the therapist is not different from any other human action in that it presupposes a certain understanding of existence. It is evident that the only understanding of existence that makes sense out of the activity of the psychotherapist is the assumption that man ought not to be neurotically guilty, anxious, hostile, and under the power of destructive compulsions. The therapist accepts the client in the midst of his guilt and compulsions not on the narrow assumption that he is just privately acceptable to the therapist as a human being but on the much more basic assumption that he is acceptable as a human being by the cosmos or the universe or by being itself and that he is intended for authentic life. *The counselor is not the source of acceptance; he only points to an acceptance that has its source beyond himself.* He assumes an acceptance that is already there, despite all human rejection. He presupposes that the individual has no ontological need of being guilty and frightened. This is simply to say that there is no final threat in life and that life is intended to be received with joy and trust in the future, love for the neighbor, and freedom from neurotic bondage. Although the therapist understands that there are, indeed, meaningful reasons why the individual is guilty, anxious, and hostile, he refuses to admit that there is any ontological ground or any basis in being itself for guilt, anxiety, and hostility. He sees neurotic behavior as meaningful behavior but without ontological grounding. He assumes that man does not know himself properly when he is neurotically guilty, frightened, and depressed. He assumes that it is written into the universe that the individual *is* acceptable.[12] This is a much more profound ontological assumption than is ordinarily acknowledged by the therapist.

The next crucial step in our argument: *This implicit assumption is precisely what is made explicit by God's self-disclosure in Jesus Christ.* The Christian kerygma seeks to state clearly and decisively that God has made himself known as one who accepts us unconditionally, that the One who gives us life is *for* us.[13] This Word is declared not in an idea but in an event. The ministry of Jesus of Nazareth is the originative event that calls forth the witness of the church to this Word from on high.

The effective counselor offers the individual the possibility for self-acceptance by accepting him as he is. But the counselor is not merely expressing his own private opinion that the individual is acceptable to him, but much more he is performing a *representative ministry,* implicitly communicating to the individual through this relationship that he *is acceptable* in the midst of his guilt. Accepted by whom or what? It is clear that it is not merely by the moral or cultural order but by creation itself or some principle in creation itself. He can therefore make all of his feelings available to awareness.

This is a theological assumption which undergirds all effective therapy. It is not just an anthropological or humanistic assumption, since it assumes an acceptance far beyond human acceptance and, as a matter of fact, in spite of radical human rejection. How does the therapist arrive at this assumption? He does not arrive at it, he assumes it from the beginning.

Christian celebration is completely unapologetic about basing its witness not on human insight but upon divine revelation. The love of God is known only through the self-disclosure of God. The event to which the church witnesses is an event that the Christian community believes makes explicit this assumption that the counseling process presupposes — that the final power in life is for

us, and that we are forgiven and acceptable. The Christ
event clarifies this assumption. In our prodigality, alienation, estrangement, frustration, guilt, and hostility we find
we are still loved by the Father and received into sonship. This divine love is not a reality we discover but a
reality that discovers us. We do not win God, he wins us.

Just as one cannot know another person until he speaks
or discloses himself to others, we, under finite and historical limitations, cannot know God until he speaks to
us and discloses himself to us. We may vaguely sense the
intuition that we are accepted by some final reality in the
midst of our lack of self-fulfillment as does the psychotherapist, but we do not fully understand divine forgiveness until it is mediated to us clearly and explicitly by
God himself in the Christ event.

It is in this way that a theology of revelation and a
therapy of insight are internally self-consistent, since the
therapy of insight already implicitly presupposes that gracious Word that is made explicit in revelation. The reason it has been assumed that there can be no dialogue
between a theology of revelation and a therapy of insight
has been that we have failed to understand this implicit
Christological assumption of therapy.

A simple syllogism captures the core of our proposal:
(a) If, in order to be effective, psychotherapy must mediate an accepting reality which is grounded in being itself;
(b) if the accepting reality in being itself has disclosed itself in an event to which the Christian proclamation explicitly witnesses; then (c) the implicit ontological assumption of all effective psychotherapy is made explicit
in the Christian proclamation.

But if this is so, what constitutes the basic difference
between therapy and proclamation? Only that the latter
attempts to make explicit what the former implicitly

assumes? Indeed that, but more so the basic uniqueness of Christian proclamation is that this word of acceptance is not merely an idea, but is allegedly made known concretely in an *event*.[14] The accepting reality, which the therapist might know vaguely as "life," has made itself fully and explicitly known in a special history, a salvation-occur-rence, which Christian worship celebrates and Christian preaching seeks to clarify. However important it may be for the patient to feel "I am accepted," this says little about the accepting reality. Christian proclamation has little that is distinctive to say about therapeutic growth except as it speaks of the self-disclosure of this accepting reality. If this accepting reality has not met us in an event, but remains merely an idea in our minds, then however much we may intuit that we are accepted, we can never really know the character of the accepting reality.

This event, which one might term "the self-disclosure of the accepting reality," is an occurrence that the Chris-tian community believes makes explicit this assumption which the counseling process presupposes. Failure to per-ceive the inner relation of these two disciplines has penal-ized them both, and caused them to avoid the benefit of genuine dialogue at the most basic level.

If our analysis is correct, and if there is a crucial rela-tion between what we are calling the implicit assumption of therapy and the explicit declaration of the kerygma, then another suggestion needs circumspectly to be made. With all due respect to the remarkable achivements of so-called "secular" psychotherapy, i.e., therapy without any consciousness of its ontological presupposition, we need to explore together whether it might be the case that the counselor who knows, understands, and celebrates the explicit witness of this special community to the self-disclosure of the accepting reality conceivably could at-

tain clearer perception of human sickness and health than
the therapist who only implicitly makes this assumption
without examining it. This question is raised in the most
tentative and modest way, with awareness of all the dangers that surround a deliberately religious orientation in
therapy.

3. PREACHING AND COUNSELING

Our inquiry has the very practical purpose of asking
whether Christian proclamation and client-centered counseling may be self-consistently practiced by one individual. The clarification of the ontology of acceptance
makes this possible. The good news, *Emmanuel*, that God
is with us and for us, which is the implicit basis of counseling, is the explicit basis of preaching: You are accepted
not of your own initiative but in fact whether you accept it or not, and called to accept your acceptability.[15]
You are elected by God's love whether or not you receive
and affirm your election. You are the son of the Father
no matter to what extent you take your inheritance and
flee to a far country. The church's witness to God's self-
disclosure is not true *because* it is validated in the clinical
experience of the therapist, but is made more edifying,
relevant, and meaningful when we see it operating in
effective therapy.

When the pastor performs his function as a counselor,
his faith is becoming active in love. Here proclamation
and therapy support one another in a total ministry of
witness and mission. The love of God to which he witnesses in preaching is recapitulated in an analogous fashion in the empathy of counseling.

Counseling enriches preaching, since participating in the
anguish, conflict, and perplexity of the parishioner enables
the minister better to understand the depths of the hu-

man predicament. Furthermore, it is clear that since the Christian proclamation strengthens self-understanding, it also strengthens counseling. We may be justly suspicious of any special claims to a special kind of religious therapy. This can become terribly irresponsible. But if the Christian witness is a witness to truth, and if God's self-disclosure does enable proper self-understanding, then it seems that the counselor who presupposes the explicit witness of the Christian community to the source of self-acceptance conceivably could have a clearer vision of the counseling process than the psychotherapist who only implicitly makes this assumption without examining it.

But why even preach, if the same accepting reality is fully present in so-called secular relationships? What is the point of talking about Jesus as the Christ, if the love that he manifests openly is hiddenly present in all of life, and perhaps uniquely and dramatically in secular psychotherapy?

The same basic issue had to be faced in the New Testament. Paul had declared that "there is no distinction between Jew and Greek; the same Lord is Lord of all and bestows his riches upon all who call upon him" (Rom. 10:12). Yet, if God is already present, why announce his presence? Paul therefore had to clarify that *the purpose of proclamation is that of calling man to an awareness of the reality of the situation in which he already exists,* the reality of God's occurring love; not to introduce God to his world, as if he were not already there, but to introduce man to himself as one who is always already claimed by God. Paul asks how men are to rely upon the accepting reality if they have never known themselves to be encountered by it (Rom. 10:13). And "how are they to believe in him of whom they have never heard?" (V. 14.) Then rhetorically he asks the witnessing community:

" And how are they to hear without a preacher? " In sum:
" Faith comes from what is heard, and what is heard comes
by the preaching of Christ." (Rom. 10:17.) Here is the
necessity of overt, clear, decisive proclamation, which
announces the accepting reality present in therapy as a
reality that has chosen to make itself known once for all
in history.

But, pursuing the other side of the issue, *if* kerygmatic
proclamation is so indispensable for the clarification of
the reality of acceptance, why should it not be imperative
for the effective therapist then to become a preacher?
For how can there be any genuinely deep self-acceptance
as long as the client is unaware of the word of divine
acceptance? The nub of this issue is whether divine acceptance must be mediated *verbally*, or whether it can be
authentically mediated unverbally through an interpersonal *relationship*. Our argument hinges on the assumption that liberating divine acceptance can be mediated
concretely through interpersonal relationships without
overt witness to its ground and source.

Admittedly the helping person who understands himself under the analogy of God's help may from time to
time point the client directly to the source of the accepting reality, but the moment he does, he ceases being a
counselor and becomes a preacher. If in rare circumstances
such a witness is deeply meaningful, even in so-called
secular psychotherapy, the therapist on such occasions
should be keenly aware that he is shifting his role radically
and may find it exceedingly difficult to shift back into
a listening, clarifying, accepting relationship, since the
intent of the kerygma is so easily distorted by the neurotic
mind. More so, he should never forget that this liberating
Word can be effectually embodied in relationships in
which language is not even necessary. The cross, for ex-

ample, is a language event, a word that is spoken (non-verbally, relationally) in an occurrence.

Is it therefore necessary for the fully functioning therapist to be aware of this explicit proclamation, or can he get along quite as well without it? Why should we not carry our argument to its seemingly logical conclusion and state that all therapists who are really serious about their therapy should ask themselves about the ontology of acceptance and seriously entertain the possibility of hearing and receiving the Christian's word about the self-disclosure of that accepting reality present in their therapy? Does not the witnessing community owe it to the therapeutic community to witness in this way?

It would be all too obvious to say that the witnessing community deeply wishes to communicate its particular word to these co-workers in human reconciliation. We think it is urgently important for them to realize God's reconciling presence in their midst, and we have reason to believe that it would support their efforts in therapy. But the more difficult thing to express is that the Christian community celebrates the occurring love of God precisely in the midst of secular processes that are *unaware* of His unique self-disclosure. We wish carefully to avoid the theologically dangerous trap that would argue that adequate counseling can only be done by professing Christians. Rather, we are called to declare something about humanistic and even agnostic therapy which the therapist cannot even say himself, i.e., that his own healing act is grounded in an accepting reality which is made known in Christian proclamation, and although the Christian community may have a deeper Christocentric perception of this process than the empiricist or secularist counselor himself, we are *not* proposing that it is necessary for him explicitly and self-consciously to affirm the

Christian's word in order to be an effective counselor, to mollify neurotic guilt, to enable self-understanding, and to guide troubled persons toward health and congruence.

Is therapy, then, some sort of incognito " Christian experience " which we receive in a secular context? Rather, it would be more accurate to say that therapy is a profoundly *human* experience which the Christian faith views in a particular way, viz., as mediating the love of God hiddenly present through interpersonal relationships.

Thus, we are compelled to take a fairly rigid view against preaching or direct proclamation of the evangel in the counseling relationship, in contrast to many otherwise excellent discussions of pastoral care (Thurneysen, Thilo, and most German discussions). Although we believe that overt verbal proclamation should not become a routine aspect of counseling, however, we do think that from time to time, on rare occasions, it is appropriate for the therapist freely and clearly to witness to the source of the accepting reality. Only the counselor can know the fitting time for such a witness amid the unique context of the particular interpersonal relationship. No rule of thumb can be given. In my experience as a counselor there have been only a few times when I have felt that this was truly appropriate, and in every case it was for some special reason only knowable in that particular moment that it became meaningful suddenly to become a witness to the divine Word. Even then, the Word must be spoken from within rather than without the individual's personal frame of reference.

Our stronger intuition, however, is to advise against frequent proclamatory intrusions in counseling. For our temptation is very much more to become moralizers, judgers, and answer givers, introjecting our viewpoint and imposing it upon troubled persons, often ineffectually, rather than allowing them the freedom to discover the covenant at the center of their own personal existence through dwelling in the presence of a person who mediates the reality of God's acceptance relationally rather than verbally.

4. Theological Method and Psychotherapeutic Aims

Undoubtedly a major obstacle in pursuing our particular conversation is the understandable revulsion of empirically oriented counselors for whom all this archaic talk about revelation is an insurmountable offense. It is necessary to be quite honest about the presuppositions upon which we are proceeding. Any Christian discussion of God can speak only of the God who has made himself known. Christian faith is not looking for God; it understands itself already to have been grasped by God.

In honestly revealing this presupposition, we are not proceeding differently from any authentic science which speaks honestly about its axioms and postulates, since all science proceeds with certain faith-presuppositions about causality, the reliability of empirical observation, the intelligibility of the universe, and many other assumptions which have been long questioned and have never been validated as proof. We are proceeding quite openly with such a presupposition, which our reader can either buy or not: that God has made himself known in an event, the central event celebrated in Christian worship and proclamation!

The task of Christian theology is to clarify the meaning of the Christian faith, faith being understood as man's affirmative response to God's self-disclosure in Jesus Christ. God himself is not the object of theological inquiry, since God is no " thing " or object to be investigated. Instead theology seeks to make intelligible the response of man to God's mighty deed of salvation. Whereas psychotherapy is a medical art, theology is a branch of the humanities whose task is that of analyzing and inquiring into the response of faith to the self-disclosure of God. *Faith can only be understood from its own center, since it is a response to an event that is only meaningful in the full sense to those who respond to it.*[16]

Theology differs from psychology of religion, which is concerned to observe and study as its object the religious affections and religious experience. Theology seeks, rather, to understand and clarify the view that faith has of its object, namely, the particular idea of God that is peculiar to Christian faith — the idea of God as revealed in Jesus Christ.[17]

Since faith has the character of *response* to God's self-disclosure, revelation and faith are logical correlates, in the sense that one cannot be understood apart from the other. Faith is man's affirmative answer to God's judging and affirming Word, and God's Word is apprehended only by him who has ears to hear. According to faith's witness to itself, it is a response to revelation and therefore cannot call forth itself out of its own initiative.[18]

Psychology of religion may be able to observe religious emotions, or to treat religiosity as its object, but it cannot see divine revelation. It is the man of faith whose eyes are open to revelation, and, according to faith's witness to itself, the possibility and motivating power of faith are given only in and with revelation and never apart from it. Theology and psychology are both agreed on this.

From the vantage point of God's deed in Jesus Christ, faith sees revelation both in nature and in history, although it does not regard either nature or history as synonymous with revelation. From the vantage point of God's deed in Jesus Christ, faith perceives the activity of

God as present in the psychiatric interview, although it does not identify or equate the activity of God with the psychiatric interview. The psychiatric interview is not an unambiguous expression of divine revelation, just as neither nature itself nor history itself is unambiguously a disclosure of the divine loving will, but Christian faith perceives in this so-called secular activity the judgment and grace of God. The Christian faith knows of no other God than the One who meets us in Jesus Christ.

The *authority* for speaking of revelation in the Christian community is fourfold: *Scriptural* truth *experienced* in life and illuminated by *reason* and *tradition*.[19] All four criteria have the character of response to God's self-bestowal. None of the four can be separated from the others or from the revelation which called them forth. None can claim exclusive priority. Faith receives this Word through a community (tradition) which moves through history bearing witness to the earliest witness of the apostolic community to this Word (Scripture); this Word becomes intelligible to one only when he symbolizes it in terms that are meaningful to himself and others (reason) and when it becomes relevant to his existing situation (experience).

We cannot base our affirmations about God's self-disclosure upon a mechanical Biblical literalism (fundamentalism), nor exclusively upon an ecclesiastical tradition that would claim to have an inerrant interpretation of it (ecclesiastical archaism), nor strictly upon its reasonableness and our rational analysis of it (rationalism), nor upon our experiencing the benefits of it (pietism). An exclusive emphasis on any one without the support of the others produces a weak and inadequate theological method.

If theology emerges essentially in response to divine

revelation, therapeutic growth emerges out of intrapersonal and interpersonal insight. By insight we mean not
merely cognitive understanding, but authentic self-per-
ception, self-awareness, and self-understanding which can
only come from truly "seeing into" oneself. If the purpose of psychotherapy is insight into oneself and one's
interpersonal relationships in order that one might come
more adequately to function amid the anxieties, guilt, and
contingencies of human existence, the purpose of theology
is clarification of faith's understanding of that divine self-
disclosure which enables the sufferer to perceive himself
and his neighbor anew from the vantage point of God's
own care and love for man amid the limitations of his
existence. Whereas insight involves the subject seeing into
something, revelation always involves something being
disclosed to the subject. In achieving insight, one *grasps*,
whereas one is *grasped* by revelation. The term "revela-
lation" is not the exclusive property of religious discourse, and may refer to anything that is disclosed or revealed.[20] In our discussion, revelation refers not to the
general usage of the term, but to that unique self-disclosure of divine forgiving love which Christian worship
celebrates. It is from the vantage point of this event that
the Christian community has come to make sense out of
other events. In this event is declared a final meaning
that illumines all other meanings, and in this sense is
revelation. In every case, revelation differs from psychotherapeutic insight in that the initiative for self-disclosure
is not within the self but comes to the self as a gift of
the initiative of another. Now we must ask how therapy
proceeds to achieve therapeutic insight.

The individual is given a safe, permissive, and supportive environment in which to explore his feelings and
work through inconsistencies that he experiences in his
behavior. The understanding of therapy that has proved

most useful in Protestant pastoral care — client-centered therapy — radically assumes the attitude that the individual has resources within himself for appropriate self-direction, if given a safe opportunity in which to explore himself.[21] It understands effective therapy not as a method by which one learns to diagnose and manipulate others, but a relationship and an attitude which radically assumes the worth of the individual and relies heavily upon his capacity for self-reorientation.

Psychotherapy belongs to an ancient tradition of philosophical insight dating back to Socrates and before, although most therapists consistently ignore their philosophical heritage, since in the effort to achieve the status of a legitimate science psychotherapy has virtually cut its roots from philosophy.[22] The Socratic method, like psychotherapy, assumed that the individual has the truth within himself, and the only function of the philosopher was to serve as a midwife to help give birth to the truth by putting questions to the knower.[23]

The burden of healing in psychotherapy is on the individual himself. He must " see into " himself in a way no other man can do for him. This process is obviously quite different both from ordinary medicine and theology. The basic assumption of therapy is given poetic form in an insightful line from *Macbeth*. In her obsessive guilt Lady Macbeth has become very sick. The Doctor has acknowledged that " this disease is beyond my practice." The impatient Macbeth asks the Doctor for a cure.

> Canst thou not minister to a mind diseas'd,
> Pluck from the memory a rooted sorrow,
> Raze out the written troubles of the brain,
> And with some sweet oblivious antidote
> Cleanse the stuff'd bosom of that perilous stuff
> Which weighs upon the heart?

The reply of Shakespeare's Doctor is the reply of our contemporary psychotherapist:

Therein the patient must minister to himself.

Psychotherapy lives out of the spirit of this great philosophical and literary tradition, of which Shakespeare and Socrates are exemplars, which knows that the cure for the sickness of the self must come from insight into oneself.

The therapist who has most meaningfully spelled out an understanding of therapy relevant to Christian proclamation has been Carl Rogers, who, instead of emphasizing special adeptness in diagnostic training, has described effective therapy essentially in terms of a relationship in which one enters into the sufferer's frame of reference, empathetically participating with him in his struggle to understand himself, clarifying his feelings and the alternatives that he sees for himself. Unlike psychoanalysis, which involves an advanced diagnostic ability that can only be the fruit of extensive training, client-centered therapy has proven itself easily adaptable by pastors and priests in the pastoral situation. If the helping task is principally that of entering into the internal dialogue of the individual, standing in his shoes, clarifying his self-expressions, and helping him consolidate the gains he makes as he achieves insight into himself, the sensitive pastor using such an approach can do very little harm and often much good. Leaders in American pastoral care have helped transpose client-centered attitudes into the pastoral context without fundamental changes. Although we owe a great debt to these men, their work needs the correction of a more serious Christology and doctrine of revelation. Few of the principal leaders in the field of pastoral counseling in America have operated out of genuinely postliberal assumptions about man, grace, and salvation. Their understanding of the therapeutic process has often been more sound, mature, and self-consistent than their theology.

5. PSYCHOANALYSIS AND OTHER THERAPIES

For readers of psychotherapeutic orientations other than client-centered therapy, we would like to explain that our discussion does not in any sense stand *against* a Freudian or Adlerian or Sullivanian point of view. Admittedly it does stand more specifically *within* the Rogerian tradition, but we wish to show that the relationship of empathetic understanding and unconditional positive regard upon which we are building our analogical study can be mediated and expressed by means of all sorts of theoretical orientations that radically differ from the client-centered pattern with which we specifically choose to deal. In this respect our discussion is strongly supported by several crucial empirical studies.

The first of these is the study in which R. W. Heine discovered that clients report similar changes in their behavior under the direction of therapists of widely variant theoretical orientations. In asking what enabled these changes, Heine found wide consensus among clients that the experience of *being understood* was the chief factor in effective therapy of whatever orientation. Consistently Heine found that the attitudinal rapport of the therapist was far more important for recovery than was the conceptual framework out of which the therapist operated.[24]

More important for our discussion, however, is the widely quoted study by Fred E. Fiedler on "A Comparative Investigation of Early Therapeutic Relationships Created by Experts and Non-Experts of the Psycho-

analytic, Non-Directive and Adlerian Schools," [25] which
strongly supports our hunch that our thesis applies also
to psychoanalysis and other psychotherapies. Fiedler's inquiry showed that expert therapists with different orientations form similar empathetic relationships with their
clients. In his related article on " The Concept of an Ideal
Therapeutic Relationship," [26] in which he was searching
for a consensus among Freudian, Rogerian, and Adlerian
therapists on the nature of effective therapy, Fiedler found
that the more *experienced* therapists, regardless of their
widely varied orientations, described the therapeutic process in quite *similar* terms. Surprisingly, there was a
greater correlation noted between *experienced* therapists
of *different* orientations than between experts and *non-
experts* of the *same* theoretical orientation. The most
characteristic aspect of the ideal therapeutic relationship
described by dissimilar therapists was that the therapist
was perceived as able to participate completely in the
client's internal communication.[27]

Sidney Jourard also emphasizes that it is not the theoretical orientation of the therapist that fosters growth but
" the manner of the therapist's *being* when in the presence
of the patient. *Effective* therapists seem to follow this
implicit hypothesis: If they *are themselves* in the presence
of the patient, avoiding compulsions to silence, to reflection, to interaction, to impersonal technique, and kindred
character disorders, but instead striving to know their patient, involving themselves in his situation, and then responding to his utterances with their spontaneous selves,
this fosters growth. In short, they love their patients. . . .
Evidently it is only the therapist's good will which needs
to be predictable, not his specific responses to a patient's
disclosures." [28]

On the basis of these studies we propose that although

we rely heavily upon Rogers as our principal theorist of therapy, our thesis can just as easily be related to the dynamics of other types of therapy, such as psychoanalysis and ego psychology, and that *an ontology of acceptance is identifiable in any truly therapeutic process.* Therefore we hope that readers who find good reason for resisting a strict client-centered approach will exercise their own ingenuity and insight to relate our series of analogies to their own understanding of effective therapy.

As an example of how this ontology of acceptance might proceed in other psychotherapies, we will single out one approach and attempt briefly to see just how the reality of acceptance, of which the therapist is merely representative, manifests itself. We choose psychoanalysis, using Freud's own description of therapy as the basis for our discussion, since virtually all modern psychotherapies are in some sense children or stepchildren of Freudian analysis, and since Freud's procedure of free association and overcoming resistance admirably illustrates our point about the necessity of a context of radical acceptance.

Note the dimension of unconditional acceptance of the client's feeling which must have been present in Freud's own instruction to his psychoanalytic patients at the beginning of the first interview: " Before I can say anything to you, I must know a great deal about you; please tell me what you know about yourself. . . . Your talk with me must differ in one respect from an ordinary conversation. . . . Say whatever goes through your mind. Act as if you were sitting at the window of a railway train and describing to someone behind you the changing views you see outside. Finally, never forget that you have promised absolute honesty, and never leave anything unsaid because for any reason it is unpleasant to say it." [29] The single-minded objective of psychoanalysis is the at-

tempt to share fully in the client's own internal experience
and to bring a cohesive interpretation of this experience
into the client's own awareness. "Thou shalt not bear
false witness" is perhaps the chief cornerstone of psychoanalytic treatment.

What essentially happens in therapy, according to
Freud? In an early essay (1905), Freud suggested three
formulas that capture the essence: (a) "remove the amnesias"; (b) "all repressions are to be undone"; (c) "the
problem consists in making the unconscious accessible to
consciousness, which is done by overcoming the resistances."[30] The aim of therapy is thus, in a word, self-
disclosure. It is the introduction of the patient to himself. It is the removal of barriers to self-encounter and
self-understanding. Such is only possible in the presence
of one who in some sense empathetically understands and
unjudgmentally accepts all that he hears.

We are arguing that Freud himself emphasized in deed,
if not in word, the accepting role of the therapist as
mediator of an acceptance rooted in reality itself. It is
only in such a context that Freud can speak of genuinely
free association of "involuntary thoughts most frequently
regarded as disturbing elements and therefore ordinarily
pushed aside. . . ."[31] Such a struggle against resistance
and overcoming of amnesias is only possible in the presence of radically accepting reality mediated through the
therapist, but not merely created *de novo* out of the
therapist's imagination or natural sympathies.

Freud significantly distinguishes his own treatment
from guidance therapy or "treatment by suggestion,"
which "achieves nothing toward the discovery of the patient's unconscious; it makes him less able than ever to
overcome the deeper resistances, and in the more severe
cases it invariably fails on account of the insatiability it
rouses in the patient, who then tries to reverse the situa-

tion, finding the analysis of the physician more interesting than his own." [32] He emphasized that "therapeutic efficacy does not lie in the suggestive prohibitive command of the physician," [33] but in the fact that symptoms automatically disappear when they are, through free association and transference, redirected from their original course of symptom formation.

Just as the patient's full self-disclosure is the precondition of psychoanalysis, so full self-awareness on the part of the therapist is the precondition of effective therapy. Freud commented on the "fundamental rule of psychoanalysis" as follows:

Just as the patient must relate all that self-observation can detect, and must restrain all the logical and affective objections which would urge him to select, so the physician must put himself in a position to use all that is told him for the purposes of interpretation and recognition of what is hidden in the unconscious, which the patient forgoes. Expressed in a formula, he must bend his own unconscious like a receptive organ towards the emerging unconscious of the patient, be as the receiver of the telephone to the disc. [34]

We believe that these passages show that psychoanalysis as well as client-centered therapy is amenable to an ontology of acceptance. For whenever the radical acceptance presupposed in free association is genuinely actualized, it is never on the mere basis of the sheer personal sympathy of the therapist, but as a representative ontological commitment, which affirms not merely that the client is acceptable privately to the analyst, but that however detestable he may be to himself and society, he is nevertheless acceptable in the universe and is being given cosmic permission for personal growth.

6. THERAPY AS SELF-DISCLOSURE

The remarkable recent findings of psychologist Sidney Jourard are most suggestive for our thesis and significant for the future course of psychotherapy. In *The Transparent Self* and related journal articles,[35] Jourard has argued that the crux of the process of psychotherapy is *self-disclosure*. Effective therapy means free, full, and meaningful self-disclosure. For the first time in the history of modern psychotherapy, we thus have been presented with a responsible theory of psychic health built around the concept of *revelation* that is a virtual synonym for self-disclosure.

"What, after all, is the situation called psychotherapy," Jourard asks, "but a situation wherein one person, the patient — alienated from himself, troubled — starts to disclose his self to the other person." [36] People need psychotherapy because "*they have not disclosed themselves in some optimum degree to the people in their life.*" [37] Jourard's empirical research allegedly supports his assertion that "*no man can come to know himself except as the outcome of disclosing himself to another person.*" [38] The resulting therapeutic dictum, Jourard's version of the Delphic oracle, becomes: Make thyself known, and then thou wilt know thyself.[39]

The importance of this thesis for our study is not that it provides startling new information on the nature of therapy,[40] but rather its unique, existential, thought-provoking style of expression and the fact that at long last we now have an empirically defended theory of personal change, however fragmentary, which is centered on a concept of self-disclosure analogous to the Christian understanding of revelation. We wish to explore the intriguing dimensions of the analogy between the divine self-disclosure in the Christ event and human self-disclosure in effective counseling. Jourard's thesis is suggestive and exciting from the vantage point of a theology of revelation for two reasons: (*a*) Therapeutic growth is alleged to be a response to the self-disclosure of another, and (b) self-disclosure is a direct linguistic equivalent to revelation, the central assumption of Christian theology.

We offer the following syllogism for the general consideration of this issue:

(1) *If genuine therapeutic growth is based upon human self-disclosure,* as Jourard's thesis suggests, and,

(2) *If authentic human self-disclosure exists as a response to divine revelation,* as the kerygma suggests, then,

(3) *The divine self-disclosure is properly the precondition of authentic psychotherapeutic growth.*

Prospectively, we would offer the following *hypothesis* for further theological and therapeutic exploration: *An adequate theory of therapy must not only understand therapeutic growth as a product of human self-disclosure, but authentic human self-disclosure as a response to the self-disclosure of God in being itself.* The kerygma announces that it is in response to the radical, full self-disclosure of God that men are most truly liberated to disclose themselves to themselves and to others. What viable analogy exists between this theological affirmation and Jourard's thesis that man is most truly freed to disclose himself to himself and others in the presence of one who discloses himself fully? Is there any illuminating analogy between the kerygma's proclamation that healthy, full-functioning authenticity finally exists as a response to the revelation of God, and Jourard's view that human health exists essentially as a response to human self-disclosure? To what extent can an acceptable theory of therapy be developed which is illuminated by and grounded in an analogy of faith that views all human self-disclosure under the analogy of divine self-disclosure in being itself?

Whatever the answers might be, at least it is clear that the essential concern of both classical Christian theology and this particular brand of clinical psychology is the same: the dynamics of self-disclosure, whether divine or human. For God is not known, according to Hebrew-Christian thought, unless and until he makes himself known, and thus the knowability of God is dependent upon his self-disclosure or revelation. If the Pentateuch, the prophets, the Fourth Gospel, Augustine, Luther, and Barth carry this argument through the whole span of the Judeo-Christian tradition, it is interesting that Jourard also argues formally in the same way regarding the knowability of the human self in psychotherapy: "You can truly know me only if I let you; only if I *want* you to know me." [41] As the kerygma announces divine revelation always as an act of sovereign divine freedom, so does Jourard speak of therapeutic self-disclosure as an unmanipulable act of human freedom: "Man's self, as near as we now know, can never be known to any save the experiencing individual unless the individual man unequivocably co-operates and makes his self known. In short, man must consent; if we would know his self, he must *want* to tell us. If he doesn't wish to tell us of his self, we can torture him, browbeat him, tempt him, even make incisive psychoanalytic guesses; but unless he wishes to make his self known, we will of course never know it." [42] As Barth criticizes all natural theologies for arguing the knowability of God apart from revelation, so does Jourard criticize all manipulative diagnostic therapies, which would presume upon the knowability of the self apart from its own free self-disclosure.

That "real-self disclosure begets real-self disclosure" is the next phase of the argument. The self is free to expose itself only in the presence of authentic self-disclosure. Thus the experienced therapist is led to confess that "*the closest I can come to eliciting and reinforcing real-self behavior in my patient is by manifesting it my-self.*" [43]

Since much psychotherapy, following the Freudian stress upon resistance, has assumed that concealment is the natural condition of man, all sorts of stratagems have been attempted by psychotherapists in order to penetrate these defenses. But Jourard argues that "recent experience and research is beginning to show that such methods . . . are unnecessary when a man *wants* to be known. Under these conditions, he will do everything in his power to make sure that the other person's image of him is as accurate as possible." [44] He chides experimental psychological researchers for having "actually fostered self-concealment and inauthenticity in our human subjects, and then reported that human subjects are notoriously duplicitous. Our psychologies of perception, of learning, of motivation, of inter-personal relations have all grown out of research where the investigator has concealed his purposes from the subject." [45]

God reveals himself because he *loves*, according to the kerygma. The motivating force behind the process of self-disclosure is *agapē*. The will of God to make himself known is the will of One who loves, and therefore loves to be known as One who loves. Likewise, in Jourard's view, genuine love motivates self-disclosure: "If I love someone, not only do I strive to know him, so that I can devote myself more effectively to his well-being; *I also display my love by letting him know me.*" [46] Ultimately Jourard confesses that love is the basic enabling reality and power of therapeutic help, arguing persuasively from empirical studies that "actively accepting, empathetic, loving, non-punitive response — in short, love — provides the optimum conditions under which man will disclose, or expose, his naked, quivering self to our gaze." [47]

This affirmation of love as the precondition of therapeutic effectiveness, however, itself needs and demands for its completion the deeper ontological context of God's own love. For it is only unconditional divine love that can ultimately provide the conditions for full and free human self-disclosure.

It is not accidental that Jourard quite unselfconsciously reaches for Biblical images to express the nature of psychotherapy as a process of *invitation to authentic being*, being oneself, dropping pretenses and defenses. "It fascinates me to think of psychotherapy as a situation where the therapist, a 'redeemed' or rehabilitated dissembler, invites his patient to try the manly rigors of the authentic way. The patient is most likely to accept the invitation, it has seemed to me, when the therapist is a role-model of uncontrived honesty." [48] If the beginning point of all Christian theology is that God has made himself known in an event that becomes the pattern and wellspring for all human self-understanding and self-disclosure, the beginning point for Jourard's theory of therapy is that when the therapist makes himself fully known in the therapeutic relationship, it becomes the pattern and wellspring for subsequent self-understanding and self-disclosure.

CHAPTER II

THE EXPLICIT PROCLAMATION
OF THE KERYGMA

Having examined the subtle ontological assumption hidden in all effective psychotherapy, we are now ready to explore, by means of a series of analogies, certain specific ways in which the explicit proclamation of the Christian kerygma illumines and clarifies the therapeutic process. Aware of the rugged imprecision of all analogical thinking, we shall later include a more detailed discussion of the limits of analogy in theological method. Now we shall merely provide a working definition of *analogia fidei,* leaving it to this later section to elaborate and defend it as a tool for theological reflection and particularly for use in developing a theology of culture.

Karl Barth has revolutionized the concept of analogy with his special exegesis of the analogy of faith (*analogia fidei*). It differs from natural theology's *analogia entis* (*analogy of being*), which begins with the concept of being, and on the assumption that man and God share in being, although imperfectly in the one case and perfectly in the other, it develops certain analogies between these two dissimilar subjects, the being of man and the being of God. We know from natural observation, e.g., that the good father loves his child. If God loves us as the good father loves his child, then we can learn something about the fatherhood of God by observing the character of good human fatherhood. So goes the process of natural theology — reading to the divine from the human on the basis of what is known about finite being.[1]

Typically, whenever analogies have been proposed between psychotherapy and theology, they have read *from* therapeutic experience *to* certain theological categories, i.e., on the basis of natural analogy attempting to derive certain theological learnings from a knowledge of psychotherapy. Up to this point, little attention has been given to *turning the analogy around* to ask what we can learn about therapy from the self-disclosure of God. Our project will consist essentially of turning the analogy around to read psychotherapy under the analogy of faith, allowing the process of empathy to be illuminated by the empathetic understanding of God in Jesus Christ.

In order to accomplish this task, we shall rely heavily upon the alternative type of analogical thinking, which actually promises to revolutionize the whole use of analogy in theological reflection, viz., Barth's analogy of faith, which, unlike natural analogies, *begins instead with God's action as it is received in faith, and views the natural relationship from the vantage point of the divine activity.*[2] For example, *first* God has met us in Jesus Christ with infinite self-giving love amid our sin, as a father loves a prodigal son, and only *therefore* can we know what authentic fatherly love means, because we have been authentically loved by God the Father. Only the eyes of faith see the analogy of faith, whereas the analogy of being intends to be visible to the natural eye of rational analysis. Although a full explication of this methodology must await explication in Chapter IV, such is the procedure that we shall employ as we seek to grapple freshly with the relation between the explicit affirmations of the

Christian kerygma and the implicit assumptions of the therapeutic process.

With this in view, we are now ready to examine a table of categories which may allow us to visualize a new approach to the conversation. If a fresh statement of the relationship is to clarify the analogy between God's mode of being in the world and the counselor's mode of being with the troubled person, the following terms must be correlated:

God's Activity (Revelation)	Therapist's Actions (Clarification)	Individual's Response (Growth Toward Authenticity)
1. Incarnation	Empathetic understanding	Increased self-understanding
2. Divine congruence	Therapeutic congruence	Increased self-identity
3. Forgiveness	Acceptance	Increased self-acceptance
4. Grace	Permissiveness	Increased self-direction
5. Divine love	Unconditional positive regard	Increased love of others

It should be clear that we are talking about varied modes of a single analogy, not five independent analogies. Although it may be useful to *distinguish* various aspects of the analogy, it is not really accurate to *separate* them as if any could stand alone, since they all interconnect in a single broad analogy in which no one aspect makes complete sense without the others.

Doubtless many more than five dimensions of this analogy could be observed and fittingly described. For example, Father Godin has already elaborated our proposal with a perceptive analogy between the divine re-

fusal to answer our neurotic supplications and the silence
of the therapist amid the neurotic demands of the client.[3]
Although we suspect that there are many more possible
dimensions of the analogy, we have limited ourselves to
five dimensions that strike us as tenable, worthy of further inquiry, and which in each case represent some
central affirmation of the Christian kerygma as analogous
to something crucial to the process of therapy.

1. Incarnation, Empathy, and Self-understanding

Empathy is the process of placing oneself in the frame
of reference of another, perceiving the world as he perceives it, sharing his world with him.[4] *Incarnation* means
that God assumes our frame of reference, entering into
our human situation of finitude and estrangement, sharing our human condition even unto death.[5]

When the troubled person finds himself under the care
of a therapist with genuine empathy, i.e., with someone
who truly seems able to share his perceptual framework,
he experiences a profoundly liberating feeling of being
known, *being understood*. Empathy is the precondition
of all therapeutic effectiveness. Self-awareness, self-acceptance, and self-direction are all blocked without the
experiencing of empathy.

Christian worship celebrates the God who has chosen
to enter our human frame of reference, to participate in
our troubled condition, and to affirm human existence by
sharing in it in all its radical contingency, suffering,
and death. Just as the counselor enters the frame of reference of the patient and fully participates in his neurosis,
without himself being neurotic, so God, according to the
Christian witness, participates concretely in our human
estrangement without himself being estranged.

We shall take special care to clarify the ambiguities

of this first analogical dimension, since it is the most representative of all the analogies. If one can clearly grasp this first analogy, the others will fall easily into place.

The heart of the first analogical dimension is the remarkable similarity, despite obvious dissimilarities, between the empathetic deed of God in the incarnation, and the *descent* of the therapist into the depths of the hell and internal conflict and alienation of the client. The characteristic response of the sufferer to genuine empathy is the profound and moving experience of being known, being deeply understood, or the feeling that a well-functioning person is going with him on his way through a frightening morass. This experience may be understood in the broader context of the characteristic response of faith to the incarnate love of God, which is prototypically celebrated in the joy of the angelic hosts of the first Christmas: Emmanuel! *God is with us.* God himself has taken up our cause! We are able to affirm our humanity, because God himself has affirmed it. We are profoundly aware of our being known, since we are known by God himself who takes our frame upon himself and shares our finitude.

When the Apostles' Creed confesses its trust in the One who was *born* of the Virgin Mary, *suffered* under Pontius Pilate, was *crucified* and *buried,* it freights a radical affirmation of God's determination to share fully in our human condition. To be born! The whole witness to the virgin birth in the late oral tradition emerged as an attack upon docetic views of the Christ event, which alleged that Christ was never really born, never fully finite and human in the fleshly sense. But the Christian confession affirms that the Incarnate Lord was *born,* suffered, was crucified. He participates in our estrangement even unto death! He was dead and buried! That it was

the Son of God of whom this ancient confession spoke
makes this a remarkable affirmation of the unconditional
sense in which God condescends to share our creaturely
frame. Elsewhere in the Christian confession we also
discover the deeply symbolic account of God's descent
into *hell* to reclaim the total brokenness of human history (Eph. 4:9). Thus the kerygma makes a radical cosmic affirmation of the very same sort of empathetic condescension or entry into another man's estrangement,
which we find fragmentarily in psychotherapy.

Although the witness to the incarnation is subject to
various distortions, it nevertheless remains central to
Christian faith, since it asserts that the Word or *logos* of
God, divine love, is historical and becomes an event (not
merely an idea) in the ministry of Jesus of Nazareth.
Christian proclamation can never begin by apologizing
for its witness to the gracious love of God, which assumes historical form. Rather, whenever the word of the
incarnation is announced, it is to be received with joy in
the spirit of celebration, or else it becomes trapped in
the worst sort of defensive apologetics. For it is nothing
less than the love of God that has met us on our own
truly human level, in the manger and the cross.

Perhaps the *locus classicus* of this kenotic, empathetic
Christology is the Pauline rendition of the ancient liturgi-
cal hymn in Philippians, in which he calls all the faithful
to " have this mind . . . which you have in Christ Jesus,
who, though he was in the form of God, did not count
equality with God a thing to be grasped, but emptied
himself, taking the form of a servant, being born in the
likeness of men " (Phil. 2:5-7). The radical character of
this self-emptying empathy (kenosis) is set forth in
these dramatic terms: " And being found in human form
he humbled himself and became obedient unto death,

even death on a cross" (Phil. 2:8). Can it be said analogically that the truly empathetic therapist who descends imaginatively into the depths of the brokenness
of the neighbor, the neurotic, the compulsively guilty,
even into the deathlike lostness of the psychotic, in some
sense "has that mind" which was in the Servant Messiah?

It is interesting to note that one of the principal Biblical images of the incarnation is that of God's *dwelling*
for a time in our midst. It is not far from the mark to
affirm likewise that there is a sense in which the psychotherapist *dwells,* makes his home for a while, in the
strange frame of reference of the alienated neighbor.
"The Word became flesh and pitched his tent among
us" or "tabernacled with us" is an alternative reading
of the famous passage in John 1:14. There is also a sense
in which the effective therapist pitches his tent in the
shifting sands of the strange inner world of the troubled
neighbor, sharing imaginatively in his human condition
for a while.

The early church's proclamation about Christ's descent
into hell constitutes the most dramatic witness to the
infinite scope of God's unconditional empathetic love.
Analogously the therapeutic process may be seen as a
certain sort of descent into hell. The therapist allows himself to engage in the depths of inner conflict of the neighbor. He descends into that hell with the neighbor, which
may in turn free the neighbor to let himself down into
the hell of his own feelings.

Paul well illustrates the basic form of the empathetic
process when he says:

For though I am free from all men, I have made myself a slave
to all, that I might win the more. To the Jews I became as a
Jew, in order to win Jews; to those under the law I became as

one under the law — though not being myself under the law —
that I might win those under the law. To those outside the law
I became as one outside the law — not being without law toward God but under the law of Christ — that I might win those
outside the law. To the weak I became weak, that I might win
the weak. (I Cor. 9:19-22a.)

Of course, Paul is here speaking of entering into the contextual, linguistic, and cultural frame of reference of the
lawless, the weak, the Gentile, the Jew, in order that
he might relevantly announce the kerygma. But a similar
process occurs in counseling, where the counselor empathetically becomes as if he were a troubled man, in
order that he might win the client back to maturity and
sanity. Paul then summarizes his mission of witness by
saying, "I have become all things to all men, that I
might by all means save some" (I Cor. 9:22). The effective therapist similarly learns a flexibility which frees him
to become all things to all men in a certain sense, i.e.,
to enter into many different perceptual orientations, that
he may bring some to health (*salvus*).

Among the synonyms of empathy listed by Katz,[6] many
are used frequently in the New Testament to describe or
clarify the involvement of God in the world. Among
these are terms such as:

becomes fully of	shares or participates in
is attuned to	responds to
abandons himself in	forgets himself in
is caught up in	is absorbed by
is immersed in	blends himself with

It is not accidental that such verbs are frequently employed by the kerygma to describe the relation of Christ
to human brokenness.[7]

Just as the incarnation witnesses to the God who does
not just diagnose or analyze man's needs but actively par-

ticipates in them, likewise effective counseling is not just objective diagnosis of the individual's conflict but active empathetic involvement in the patient's suffering. Certain forms of therapy that rely essentially on diagnosis are perhaps less analogous to the incarnation than are client-centered therapies in which the counselor actively seeks the frame of reference of the other individual. If the counselor tries to get the client into his frame of reference, imposing upon him a diagnostic scheme that may be foreign to his private world, or if the analyst tries to explain the client to himself on the assumption that he knows better what the client needs than the client himself, this indicates a limited participation in the situation of the client. In more client-centered approaches, however, the counselor divests himself of his own point of view and by a process of kenosis or self-emptying enters fully into the private and subjective world of the client.[8] To the theologian this is much more suggestive of the pattern of the incarnation than diagnostic approaches.

The analogy breaks down, of course, at certain crucial points. The therapist's understanding is not divine understanding.[9] His capacity to enter the individual's situation is always limited by his own historical perspective, cultural prejudices, and parataxic distortions. The counselor may be totally unaware of the Christian kerygma concerning the divine Word of which his work is an analogue. When effective, however, he himself is nevertheless existentially involved in a process which embodies that Word.

One major point at which the analogy cannot be followed is that, according to the kerygma, God takes our sin and estrangement upon himself. He does not merely share *imaginatively* in our predicament; he *substitutes* his wholeness for our brokenness. A whole set of atonement images from the priestly traditions are here pressed to service to speak of God as a sacrificial lamb ransomed for us, and one who takes our estrangement upon himself. The therapist does not propose to take anyone's sin or estrangement upon himself. He does not substitute himself or suffer for the client, except in a limited sense and as he is often paid dearly for it. The redemptive image is not nearly so radical in therapy as in God's atoning deed. The therapist only proposes to help the individual understand himself amid his suffering, not to suffer for him. So there is a limited participation in suffering, whereas in the Biblical witness there is a thoroughgoing affirmation of the divine vicarious acceptance of suffering for sin, an affirmation upon which the whole Anselmic theory of the atonement is based.

Whereas social psychologists might define empathy as taking the *role* of another, the kerygma speaks of God as not merely taking our role of humanity, but *embodying* humanity, sharing our weakness, tempted as we are, yet without sin. There is a question as to whether the *as if* quality of empathy is preserved in the incarnation. For it is not merely asserted that God becomes *as if* he were as man (a heretical Christology), but that God becomes *vere homo*.[10] This question must be more fully pursued in the next analogy between divine congruence and therapeutic congruence.

2. Divine Congruence, Therapeutic Congruence, and Self-identity

The heart of this second dimension of the analogy is this: God does not cease being himself in the midst of his sharing in human estrangement. God does not lose his identity in the midst of his incarnate involvement in the world. For precisely amid his condescension to share our humanity, he maintains his deity and his divine integrity as God — holy, sovereignly free, living Lord.[11]

The analogy sharpens: *Even as God participates in our estrangement without being estranged from himself, likewise the therapist participates in the estrangement of the client without losing his self-identity.* The effective therapist continues to feel his own feelings, to be himself, to experience this remarkable self-relation which Rogers calls congruence, wherein one's self-concept resonates with present experience. In the midst of feelings of hostility, anxiety, guilt, and value negations of all sorts, the congruent therapist does not cease to be at one with himself, reconciled with his own feelings, hiding nothing from himself, engaging in no self-deception or evasion of his own feelings.

Likewise, God continues to be at one with himself amid his radical participation in our estrangement. There is a kind of divine self-affirmation and self-knowledge which is an aspect of the *gloria Dei,* in which the incarnate Lord continues to *be himself* as God, in a way curiously illuminating for the whole concept of therapeutic congruence.

The client who senses the inner congruence of the therapist, who knows he is in the presence of one who is in touch with himself and experiences himself fully as he encounters estrangement, may be powerfully awakened to the possibility of congruence with himself. Meeting a living embodiment of self-reconciliation (albeit of a limited, imperfect order), the client nevertheless becomes newly aware of the promise of reconciliation with himself, openness to himself, which may have seemed an impossibility before therapy. The very process of dwelling for a time in the presence of a congruent person is

itself undoubtedly a healing force. Likewise in being
confronted by the kerygma's witness to the unity of the
triune God, of the God that has shared our estrangement
without himself being estranged, then we become awakened to the new possibility of affirming the human condition, as it is given with all its creaturely limitations, as
God's gift. If God can participate in human estrangement
without himself being estranged, then perhaps we too can
feel much more at home in this awesome universe.

Congruence is defined by Rogers as the state in which
" self-experiences are accurately symbolized, and are included in the self-concept in this accurately symbolized
form." [12] Synonyms of congruence are: integrated, whole,
genuine. One is congruent when he feels his feelings
clearly, is fully aware of his present experiences, and
symbolizes his feelings adequately. In order to be of
much help, a counselor to some extent must embody this
congruence between self and experience, and be perceived by another as congruent. If congruence is as important to the therapeutic process as Rogers insists,[13] it
deserves careful attention in our series of analogies. We
are asking whether there is any appropriate way to view
the experience of therapeutic congruence from the unique
vantage point of the kerygma's affirmation of the congruence of God.

Ancient trinitarian formulas bear curious parallels to
the carefully worded, painfully constructed language of
modern descriptions of empathy, such as those by Reik
and Katz, in which much attention is given to making
clear that the empathetic process does not imply the negation of one's own selfhood or identity. The somewhat
unwieldy trinitarian categories sought to clarify the dynamics of God's self-relation, in effect arguing for the
congruence of the incarnate God, that God the Father

does not cease being God when he becomes God the Son who participates in the human condition. The God who creates us is indeed the same One who chooses to embody our human condition without ceasing to be God. The deeper intention of this complex fourth-century vocabulary is to affirm the incarnate love of God without denying the unity, integrity, and holiness of God. Although such trinitarian language appears somewhat mystifying to the modern reader unless he is well schooled in the nuances of patristic Greek and Latin, and in Neoplatonic philosophy, nevertheless its basic dialectic is not different from some of the recent formulas for empathy and congruence proposed by Rogers, Katz, Buber, and others. Katz, for example, speaks of empathy as a " dialectic between the actual me and the me which is identified with the other person, . . . a paradoxical process in which we are at the same time fully absorbed in the identity of the other and yet capable of an experience of ourselves as separate personalities." [14] This is not substantially different from trinitarian dialectics. Reik describes the process by which the therapist learns to share " the other's experience and yet remain above the struggle." [15] Others speak of a kind of " pendulum swing " between other-identification and self-identity, or between sharing in the situation of the other without losing one's own self-awareness. Although the pendulum image has no precise analogue in a dyophysite Christology, nevertheless the process of empathy as the " oscillation between identification and detachment " or a " balancing of involvement and disengagement," [16] is very suggestive of the kerygmatic affirmation about God's involvement in the human situation without self-loss or self-negation.

Rogers has defined empathy as the process of " perceiving the internal frame of reference of another with accuracy, and with the emotional components and meanings which pertain thereto, as if one were the other person, but without ever losing the 'as if' condition." [17] If the central meaning of divine congruence is that God has dramatized his freedom to enter our frame of reference, to perceive it with accuracy, to share human existence with us, yet without ever denying himself his deity, holiness, and transcendence, i.e., without ever losing the " as if " condition necessary for true participation with another, then the dialectic is remarkably similar.

Empathy is undermined if one loses the " as if " condition. Just as when the actor who really thinks he *becomes* the character he is portraying ceases to be a good actor, likewise the therapist who loses his own identity in his imaginative participation with the other is not really empathizing. The identification of which we speak in therapeutic empathy is always strictly an imaginative identification.

Analogously the early church sensed the danger of a monophysitic (one nature) Christology which would imply that God cannot in the full sense be God if he is man, or that the God-man cannot in the full sense be man if he is God incarnate, a position consistently rejected as heresy by the church fathers. God, according to Chalcedon, is *vere homo* and *vere Deus* without ceasing to be one or the other. The church fathers at Chalcedon confessed Christ as " very God and very man . . . made in all things like unto us, sin only excepted; begotten of his Father before the worlds according to his Godhead; but in these last days for us men and for our salvation born into the world." [18] No less determined was the Council of Ephesus in A.D. 431 to repudiate anyone who denied that " the Word of God suffered in the flesh, that he was crucified in the flesh, and that likewise in that same flesh tasted death." [19] Again in A.D. 680 the Council of Constantinople reaffirmed that Christ "endured our sufferings . . . not in appearance only but in very deed." [20] It was unquestionably the opinion of the church fathers that this dialectic had to be maintained in its most delicate and exact form or very disastrous theology would ensue.

Likewise the razor's edge must be maintained in the therapeutic dialectic between empathy and congruence. The therapist does not become a neurotic. If he empathizes with the paranoic who may be afraid of someone poisoning his bath water, he does not himself become afraid of poisoning. He does not have to embody that fear in order to participate with him, share his suffering, and be a redemptive factor in his recovery. In fact, he can only helpfully share in the psychotic's suffering if he has the sane capacity imaginatively to become *as if* he were a paranoic without being paranoic. Likewise the kerygma does not announce that God has become a sick, sadly neurotic man. God becomes fully man, yes, but without sin, estrangement. In Tillich's phrase, he participates fully in our estrangement without himself being estranged. [21]

Although the term empathy is a modern coinage which does not occur in the Biblical witness, the Greek word *sympatheō* does occur in a passage where Christ is celebrated as a great high priest who reconciles our estrangement:

For we have not a high priest who is unable to sympathize with our weaknesses, but one who in every respect has been tempted as we are, yet without sinning. Let us then with confidence draw near to the throne of grace, that we may receive mercy and find grace to help in time of need. (Heb. 4:15-16.)

Or to put it in a different language, Christian worship does not celebrate some God who does not participate in

our condition, but one who in *every respect* has shared
our human estrangement, yet without separation from
himself as the ground of being.

Therapeutic congruence is always an imperfect opera-
tion, however, whereas the divine congruence is alleged
to be an eternally perfect correspondence of God with
himself, of God the Father with God the Son, of God as
the Creator and Redeemer. The self-awareness of God
can admit of no imperfection. But just as human self-
understanding is always limited and imperfect, so is human self-awareness. Thus, again we must clearly limit
our analogy so as to avoid strictly the implication that
we are dealing with a univocal correspondence. We are
discussing certain identifiable similarities between two
radically different subjects, the perfectly congruent God
and the imperfectly congruent human brother. Any interpretation that would leave the impression otherwise
must be decisively repudiated.

3. Forgiveness, Acceptance, and Self-acceptance

Forgiveness means that God accepts us radically. We
are called to accept our acceptance, despite our feelings
of inacceptability. Divine forgiveness does not mean that
our phoney human existence is somehow magically
changed into utopia, but to the contrary that we are
accepted *amid* our phoniness! Nor does it mean that the
accepting reality affirms our *sham* and pretense, but that
we are affirmed *in spite of* our sham and pretense. Similarly, the therapist does not affirm neurosis. He does not
like sickness. He affirms the *person* who is wrestling with
neurotic compulsions *amid* his sickness and *in spite of* his
pretenses, distortions, projections, and absurdities in order that he might bring more of his experience into con-
scious awareness and acceptance. Just as the precondition

of self-understanding is being understood, the precondition of *self-acceptance* is genuinely being accepted. There is a significant analogy between the radical divine acceptance which is the subject of the Christian kerygma and the radical therapeutic acceptance which enables the client to accept himself.[22] As divine love recognizes and forgives the inconsistencies, the egotism and willful rebelliousness of man, and presents him with a new possibility of self-understanding, counseling likewise involves the bringing to awareness of inconsistencies within the self with the hope that they can be understood, accepted, and resolved.

In this connection let us carefully consider the implications of Paul's astonishing statement: "I know and am persuaded in the Lord Jesus that nothing is unclean in itself; but it is unclean for any one who thinks it is unclean" (Rom. 14:14). We do dishonor to the Creator by regarding anything in the created order as in itself unclean and to be rejected. Note the remarkable correlation with the therapist who welcomes into his own consciousness all sorts of otherwise ugly, dark, vulgar, immoral, twisted, frightened, and hostile feelings which are being experienced by the troubled neighbor. Such openness is given ontological grounding in the kerygma, which announces that since God has accepted his creation, we too can. It is because God has made his acceptance known in an event that we are now finally freed to acknowledge that nothing in creation is unclean in itself. Such an attitude is not a mere projection or a humanistic affirmation, but a response to nothing less than God's own self-disclosure.

The psychotherapeutic injunction that the basis for acceptance of others is self-acceptance has its deeper ontological root in the Christian proclamation that the basis for the freedom to love the neighbor is the forgiveness of God. Christian worship views the problem and possibility of acceptance in a richer dimension, since it celebrates the veritable revelation of the accepting reality in a way which makes authentic self-acceptance eternally possible. Man values himself anew in the light of God's astounding valuation of him (loved as sinner).[23] The basis of self-acceptance is divine acceptance of the self fragmented by guilt and despair and hostility. Such a Christological humanism is a deeper affirmation of man than the often shallow romanticist humanism that undergirds much psychotherapy.

The counselor's relation to the client is very different from ordinary human relations, since in addition to the positive acceptance of all feelings, there is a corresponding absence of any threat or judgmental quality. Although *judgment* of idolatries is a constant factor present in all effective psychotherapy, the source of the judgment is always the troubled individual himself. His capacity for appropriate and realistic self-criticism increases as he confronts the accepting reality mediated by the therapist. Likewise the word that God speaks is very different from all other words we hear. It is a word of permission and grace.[24] The capacity to obey God's demand increases only as we receive the reality of God's forgiving love. The gospel is not another demand upon us or law for us to obey, but first of all good news of God's forgiving verdict on our behalf, and only then and in that sense a requirement upon us to become who we are as forgiven, reconciled men. If acceptance is a universally explicit theme in modern psychotherapy, and the necessity for self-acceptance is well recognized by widely varied types of therapy,[25] the affirmation of an unconditional acceptance by the ground of being itself even and precisely *amid* all human rejection is a theme that has been little treated by therapists and then only in the most vague and uncritical manner. If it could be brought to explicit awareness, it would immensely strengthen the dialogical possibilities of therapy and theology.

In therapy, just as in divine forgiveness, the individual comes both to be more comfortable with himself and ironically to see his alienation from himself in a deeper dimension. He comes to be more aware of both his predicament and the possibility for overcoming it. He comes with more clarity to see who he *is* and who he *ought* to be, to experience himself more spontaneously and to perceive his lack of spontaneity, to be himself more completely and to sense his estrangement more deeply. As his idolatries fall and his gods are found to have clay feet, he paradoxically comes to value himself more highly.

Such a paradoxical dialectic may be viewed under the analogy of the kerygmatic affirmation that we are loved by God as sinners, and that repentance and faith are two sides of the same coin. In the language of the Christian community, fallen creation is understood as redeemed in its fallenness — *simul justus et peccator* — at once justified and sinful, and accepted precisely amid its sinfulness. The process of destruction of idolatries thus proceeds simultaneously with the rebuilding of the foundations of the authentic self.

Rogers speaks of the curious paradox that "When I accept myself as I am, then I change. . . . We cannot move away from what we are, until we thoroughly *accept* what we are." [26] If the precondition for human renewal in therapy is radical self-acceptance and honesty with oneself amid self-deceptions, in corresponding Christian language repentance constitutes the first movement toward authenticity and faith. Prior to therapy, just as prior to faith, the self is often trapped in a moral perfectionism in which there exists a great distance between "is" and "ought." During the process of therapy is and ought move toward each other. The self's ideal image is reduced in a more realistic direction and the capacity for achieving the ideal increases.[27] Similarly in Christian existence, the self who lives under grace no longer feels the tyranny and wrath of the law, but is freed by the forgiveness of God to fulfill the law in love by responding freely to the love of God.

The analogy of acceptance may be spuriously over-pursued, however, since the therapist remains a finite human brother with needs, projections, and distortions of his own. However much his functioning may mediate an accepting reality beyond himself, it always does so inadequately. Since he is a time-bound creature of history, he always operates from within the narrow bounds of his finite, cultural, and personal perspective. To ask that his acceptance perfectly reflect the unqualified Yes of divine forgiving love is to ask too much. Thus, while maintaining the character of the analogy as a statement about the similarity of two dissimilar subjects, we must repudiate the temptation to press the analogy in the direction of a univocal equation.

4. Grace, Permissiveness, and Self-direction

If revelation has the character of a *gift* that comes from beyond the resources of the individual, then we may say that in a sense psychotherapeutic healing comes to the individual as grace, since the resolution of compulsive conflict is seldom achived alone. Amid all the therapist's talk about the individual's capacity for self-direction, it nevertheless is necessary for the counselor to be there and perform his function in order for healing to be achieved.[28] The neurotic must have the help of another who can act as a midwife to that knowledge which he already has (buried) within himself. So the dynamics of healing are not wholly unlike that which the Christian community calls grace.

Effective psychotherapy places man in a new relationship to himself. He discovers a safe situation in which he is freed to be himself more fully. This situation seeks to bear no word from on high. That is not its purpose. In fact its purpose is hampered when "preaching" is inserted into the conversation from the "outside" of the individual's own unique frame of reference. The kerygma also presents man with a new possibility for self-understanding. But the two possibilities are of a different order. Both may tend toward a more appropriate self-understanding, but they are as different as insight and revelation.

The need for a genuinely permissive setting in which the individual can experience the exercise of his emerging freedom under safe conditions is widely recognized by therapists. The neurotic individual, whose capacity for self-determination has long been frustrated by destructive inner compulsions, needs a safe context for self-exploration of his feelings and for experimentation with his freedom.

Under the conditions of neurosis, the individual's attempts at genuine self-direction are continually being frustrated by a distorted, idealized self-understanding, by bizarre feelings of insecurity, guilt, and aggression. He may wish to be free to move toward the goals that he has chosen, but he cannot seem to actualize his authentic intention. However we may rightly emphasize the irrepressible tendency of the organism toward self-actualization, the neurotic individual needs *help* in order for him to actualize this original capacity. The client cannot achieve his genuine intention alone, else he would not be coming for help.

Under the conditions of a permissive setting, the individual can perceive himself *amid* his inconsistencies (enabled by the counselor's empathy), accept those inconsistencies (since he perceives them as acceptable to the therapist), and begin experimentally to exercise his freedom to move toward self-chosen goals. He learns to trust his organism to carry him toward his actual intention. He is enabled by the permissive context not only to work imaginatively through future possibilities but to work retrospectively through past conflicts and guilts. Most of all, he experiences, perhaps for the first time in his life, an environment in which he is *permitted* simply to be himself, to feel his feelings, and to learn to what degree he can expect himself to be a well-functioning person.

Similarly, the Christian community perceives the individual under the conditions of *estrangement* (from himself, others, and the One who gives him life) as incapable of actualizing his authentic freedom because of a distorted self-understanding and profound feelings of guilt and anxiety which, in effect, put his will "under bondage," i.e., in prison to spurious compulsive needs. He may intend to will to do what he perceives to be good but finds himself doing the opposite.

Under the conditions of *grace*, the individual learns to actualize his freedom, as it were, within the context of the safety of divine accepting love. The individual experiences a profound sense of divine *permission* to be who he *is*.[29] Under the conditions of grace, one may now perceive himself anew amid his human condition of finiteness (since God himself has chosen to affirm that limitation and suffering by sharing in it). He may receive this creaturely condition as the gift of the Creator, despite his moral inadequacies and pretenses (since God himself has accepted him amid his inauthenticity). He may therefore begin to learn a new way of being in the world, to exercise the freedom to be himself under the permission of divine grace, to direct himself toward goals he chooses in the light of God's liberating love. Although the doctrine of grace is easily distorted into licentious antinomianism, mechanical determinism, or irresponsible quietism, it nevertheless remains a central feature of the Christian understanding of free self-determination.

The core of this fourth analogical dimension is *the similarity, despite all other dissimilarities, between the grace of God which permits us to be who we are, calling us to self-direction under this permission, and the permission of the therapist who places the distraught person in a setting that enables and calls him to discover himself, feel his feelings, and move toward self-direction.* If the characteristic response of the man of faith to the gracious permission of God is the new experience of freedom to explore the meaning of his destiny under grace, likewise the richest benefit of therapeutic permissiveness is that one can test and exercise his newly discovered freedom under safe conditions of non-threat.

Again this dimension of the analogy is not to be viewed as an independent analogy, but as one unique dimension of a many-faceted analogy between the action of God and the therapeutic process. As permissiveness is misunderstood when separated from empathetic understanding, so is divine grace misunderstood if separated from the kerygma's witness to the humanity and deity of God, the acceptance and love of God in Jesus Christ.

Grace is not merely an idea but an event. It is an eschatological event which eternally happens in human history because it happens once for all in the Christ event. Grace is therefore the context in which all human decision is made, according to Christian self-understanding, whether one is aware of it or not. Growth toward authenticity may be understood as growth in the process of awareness of the grace which is present without that awareness. We are asserting that therapeutic permissiveness has its deeper ontological basis in the grace of God, which: (a) prepares the way for growth toward authenticity (prevenient grace); (b) renders a verdict upon all our inauthenticity, the crux of which is that God takes upon himself responsibility for all the brokenness of creation (justifying grace); and (c) continues to nurture and guide the new self toward the full embodiment of authentic humanity (sanctifying grace). Although this broad doctrine of grace does not have precise and elaborate parallels in the psychotherapeutic process, it is at least clear that at the center there exists an illuminating analogy between the liberating context for human fulfillment in eucharistic existence and the permissive context for personal growth in therapy.

It is " for freedom," Paul writes to the church at Galatia, "Christ has set us free" (Gal. 5:1). When we lay hold of this freedom, thrusting ourselves trustfully toward the future, "when we cry, 'Abba! Father!' it is the Spirit himself bearing witness with our spirit that we are children of God" (Rom. 8:15-16). It is God himself who bears witness within our inner selves that amid our troubled groanings we are his children, heirs of Christ, and intended for authentic life. If so, the process of therapeutic permissiveness is not fully understood merely on the level of humanistic interaction, although it certainly must be understood at that level. For God himself joins with us in our groanings to bear witness to our true humanity. The spirit we have received in the kerygma is not a "spirit of slavery leading you back into a life of fear," guilt, emptiness, and neurotic anxiety, "but a Spirit that makes us sons, enabling us to cry 'Abba! Father!' In that cry the Spirit of God joins with our spirit in testifying that we are God's children" (Rom. 8:15-16, NEB).

Thus when Paul speaks of the whole creation "groaning in travail" and "waiting with eager longing" for consummation, he adds:

Likewise the Spirit helps us in our weakness; for we do not know how to pray as we ought, but the Spirit himself intercedes for us with sighs too deep for words. And he who searches the hearts of men knows what is the mind of the Spirit. (Rom. 8:26-27.)

Who is it that truly searches the hearts of men? The psychotherapist? Certainly the therapist does. But it is God the Holy Spirit, who, according to Christian proclamation, searches "our inmost being" (NEB). For we do not know how to disclose ourselves as we ought, even in interpersonal communication. We often do not know how to overcome resistances in therapy. But we are being led in the midst of an accepting reality to which the therapist's acceptance merely points.

The sighs too deep for words are well known to any practicing counselor. Any experienced therapist knows long moments in which there is no room or time for words, amid the depths of interpersonal and intrapersonal communication. Such is the context in which an explicit Christian self-understanding celebrates the Spirit of God as our helper amid the helplessness of our own external communication.

But is Protestant theology seriously ready to affirm that alienated man in his fallenness still possesses the capacity

to reorient himself toward appropriate ends? Yes and no.
It is the hallmark of man's fallenness that he does not
know himself as fallen.[30] But the therapeutic situation
helps to teach him of his brokenness. It is in a sense a
school for repentance — a kind of secularized confessional. But the possibility for repentance (i.e., knowledge
of oneself as anxious, guilty, separated from authentic
life) is not found in isolation, but only as the *gift* of a
relationship. Therapy is not isolated self-help, but always
self-help in relation to another helper, just as Socratic
learning of the truth involves another functioning as midwife to the knower so that he might give birth to the
truth within him.

Although in this discussion we have often emphasized
self-understanding, self-acceptance, and self-direction in
order to lead one perhaps to suspect that we are essentially concerned with an intrapersonal rather than interpersonal therapy, such is certainly not our intention, since
the self is always properly understood only in its encounter with others and in fact exists only in relation with
other selves. Consequently if the self can be defined only
interpersonally, an authentic self-understanding would
already mean an understanding of oneself as bound to,
limited by, and called to serve others. That human selfhood is essentially *Mitmenschlichkeit* (a humanity with
others) is a presupposition shared by an astonishing va-
riety of therapists (Adler, Sullivan, May), social psychologists (Durkheim, Mannheim, Cooley, Mead), phi-
losophers (Heidegger, Sartre, Jaspers), and theologians
(Barth, Bultmann, Buber).

One qualification is necessary: the situation of permissiveness involves a *special*, unique healing relationship
which is not common to ordinary human relationships,
perhaps to be likened to a hospital as distinguished from

life itself. The world is not permissive. It contains all sorts of threats and value negations. So the therapeutic context exists as a special setting of permission to nurture freedom in order that it can move toward the estranged world and in the midst of it, growing and strengthening as it goes, without losing its self-directing, self-determining character amid estrangement.

If the therapists are (understandably) somewhat embarrassed to hear theologians compare their actions with God's, we wish to note that they would rightly be horrified if such a proposal were made without qualification. We are less concerned to say that God is like the therapist than that the therapist (perhaps even unwittingly) shares in the reality of God's healing in the midst of his work, and thus embodies that healing power. So as with all analogies we must not construe this as an equation, as if to suggest that therapeutic permissiveness and divine grace are synonymous, since the therapist's permission to the patient to "be himself" is a contingent event happening at one particular point in history, whereas permission of divine grace is constantly renewed as eternally given in each moment.

5. DIVINE LOVE, UNCONDITIONAL POSITIVE REGARD, AND LOVE OF OTHERS

Rogers describes unconditional positive regard as "a warm caring for the client — a caring which is not possessive, which demands no personal gratification. It is an atmosphere which simply demonstrates 'I care'; not 'I care for you *if* you behave thus and so.'" [31] How does the kerygma's witness to the *agapē* of God illuminate the ontological basis of the attitude of unconditional positive regard and provide the basis for an analogy in terms of which it is most deeply perceived?

The heart of the fifth dimension of the analogy is that *even as God unconditionally loves the sinner in order to free him from the self-righteousness, anxiety, guilt, and defensiveness that prevent him from loving his neighbor, so in effective therapy does the client experience in some sense what appears to be a relationship of unconditional positive regard, which frees him to value others anew in the light of his new self-valuation.*

An axiom shared by both psychotherapy and theology is that the precondition of loving others is understanding that one is loved.[32] The most persistent problem in following the Biblical command to love others as ourselves is, in fact, that we do not know how to love ourselves authentically, and thus cannot adequately love others after the pattern of an inadequate self-love. As the individual in effective therapy comes to perceive himself as genuinely valued and cared for by another, he increasingly finds himself freed to value and care for others. This corresponds with the basic Christian affirmation that " in this is love, not that we loved God but that he loved us. . . . If God so loved us, we also ought to love one another " (I John 4:10-11).

The *analogia fidei* reads the correspondence more precisely as follows: as we learn from divine love the character of authentic unconditional positive regard, which frees its recipient to love as he has been loved, so may we perceive in the therapeutic relationship a reflection and mediation of this divine love which is present in being itself (Col. 1:17) as the liberating ground of all human love. The client recognizes in his relationship with the therapist what seems to be an unconditional positive regard for him precisely *amid* his inconsistencies and compulsions, so as to liberate him to reflect that regard in his relationships with others. Although the therapist's positive regard is never finally *unconditional,* in the most serious sense of that word, and is often hedged about by such obvious conditions as fees, time, safety, etc., nevertheless the client *experiences* it as unconditional, since in one way or another it mirrors and representatively mediates the truly unconditional positive regard present in reality itself and made known in the Christ event.

A central theme of theological ethics is that appropriate human action exists as a *response* to the action of God.[33] If God is the only final good known in Christian ethics (Luke 18:19, " Why do you call me good? No one is good but God alone."), our human goodness can only consist in participation in the goodness of God. The effective counselor is implicitly, although not self-consciously, manifesting this Christian ethic, by entering into the situation of his neighbor and participating in his estrangement, so as to free him to love as he has been loved. Often we are reminded by the Biblical witness that love is mediated not in mere words, but principally through relationships. The New Testament enjoins, " Let us not love in word or speech but in deed and in truth " (I John 3:18). Likewise the therapeutic process is properly not merely a verbal witness to love, but the embodiment of love in and through a relationship.

As in all analogies of God and man, the analogy between divine love and therapeutic positive regard is not to be construed as an assertion of synonymity, since the positive regard of the therapist is never finally *unconditional,* however much the client may experience it as such. As a finite being with certain needs and limits of his own (conditions!), the therapist at best is only capable of making roughly transparent through the interpersonal relationship the truly unconditional positive regard rooted in reality itself.

Of the five analogical dimensions we have discussed, the first two (empathy and congruence) are easily distinguishable, but the last three (acceptance, permissiveness, and unconditional positive regard) seem much more deeply intermeshed and indistinguishable. It is not surprising also that the last three corollary theological terms (forgiveness, grace, and love) are harder to differentiate than the first two dimensions of the analogy (on the humanity and deity of God). Thus, one remaining task is to clarify some of the differences between these last three interrelated dimensions of the analogy and to defend our decision to spell out the analogy with categories that often seem similar if not actually identical.

However interdependent they may be, we wish to show that unconditional positive regard and acceptance are not synonymous. Acceptance means to be open to and to receive the contents of the other's consciousness. It would be quite possible to experience a bland relationship of acceptance without unconditional positive regard for the neighbor. For acceptance merely involves admitting another's feelings into one's own perceptive mechanism without judgmental attitudes, whereas unconditional positive regard includes the much more active affirmative aspect of prizing and reaching out for the neighbor in positive love, concern, sympathy, and care.

There is a similar passive-active distinction between the forgiveness and love of God. That God *forgives* us in the midst of our sin is essentially a verdict rendered on the sinful circumstances created by human initiative, a negation of our value negations, whereas the proclamation that God *loves* mankind in the Christ event speaks of the vigorous initiative of God which reaches out actively and positively for estranged human history. Admittedly these are two interrelated nuances of a single reality, the *forgiving love* of God, but they are distinguishable.

Simpler to distinguish, however, is the concept of unconditional positive regard from the concept of permissiveness. For permissiveness has to do essentially with the therapeutic environment that is thrown around the troubled person in order that he will have room to move imaginatively, to explore, to test himself out as a newly growing human being. Although unconditional positive regard is a crucial component of this liberating environment, it differs from permissiveness in its active, positive, seeking character.

The grace of God, as distinguished from the forgiving act of pardon, likewise has to do more broadly with the whole contextual environment of the providential action of God whereby human freedom is nurtured even amid the conditions of estrangement. Grace can be distinguished from forgiveness and love only in an abstract way, since the pardon of God is an act of grace, motivated by love. Even as it is out of his *love* for the estranged creature that God renders the verdict of forgiveness of sin, likewise (reading analogically from faith), it is nothing less than the unconditional positive regard of the therapist which nonverbally mediates a sort of " pardoning verdict " which should be implicit from the very beginning of therapy, in which it is made known (if not in words, then in relationships) that the person is prized without judgment. Although not verbalized as an act of absolution, such a verdict nevertheless remains an implicit cornerstone of the therapeutic edifice.

In each of our five analogical dimensions we have either used or implied the term *covenant ontology*, suggesting that there are hidden ontological assumptions behind the therapeutic process which are clarified in faith's response to revelation. Although the importance of the concept of

covenant ontology for our discussion is heightened by the
fact that it appears in the subtitle of this presentation, we
have not clarified either the meaning of ontology or covenant, or why these two seemingly disparate terms are
bound together in a single phrase. Our task is now briefly
to make this needed clarification.

"Ontology" means the study of being, or inquiry into
the nature and modes of being. "Covenant" means the
relation that God has chosen and established with the
world and man, as seen prototypically in the history of
the people of Israel and therefore representatively with
all creation, embracing all being, the essential terms of
which are: "They shall be my people, and I will be their
God" (Jer. 32:38). Covenant ontology is therefore a study
of being which sees being as existing in covenant and the
covenant of God as the center and circumference of being.

We are following such distinguished authorities as Eich-
rodt, Mendenhall, and Snaith in regarding covenant as the
principal overarching category of Biblical theology, embracing both the Old and New Testament witness to the
relation of God and man. The covenant love of God is celebrated in the Old Testament essentially in the form of
promise, and in the New in the form of fulfillment. Although the limitations of our discussion do not permit a
full-length elaboration of the concept of covenant, we can
at least acknowledge that the viewpoint that has framed
our inquiry has been deeply shaped by the discussion of
covenant creation in Karl Barth's *Church Dogmatics*, Volume III, and we can in good conscience refer the reader
to that remarkable presentation for a further elaboration
of the view of covenant which is here presupposed. Although Barth does not employ the term covenant ontology, the notion that all being is always already covenant
being, that covenant is the center of creation, and that the

meaning of being is only fully disclosed in Jesus Christ, is basic to his whole theological effort. Although Bonhoeffer and Teilhard de Chardin are perhaps the most brilliant proponents of a covenant ontology in the twentieth century, this orientation toward being reaches deeply into the wellsprings of the Judeo-Christian tradition, from the priestly source of the Pentateuch through the Psalms, the Johannine and Pauline epistles, to Irenaeus, Augustine, and others. Such a view of being is urgently needed to undergird and clarify the ontological assumption and the ontic commitment of the effective psychotherapist.

It is also necessary to point out that the subtitle for our discussion does not in any sense propose that we are here presenting a fully developed covenant ontology for psychotherapy, but rather that we are only attempting to take some initial steps *toward* such a project, which if properly developed might reasonably involve the best efforts of a whole generation of clinicians who seek to understand the depth dimension of their therapeutic work theologically. We are not merely suggesting, however, that a covenant ontology *must* be developed *de novo* for psychotherapy, as if it did not already exist in an implicit form. Nor are we arguing in a hortatory fashion that we *ought* to develop such a concept, or that it would be useful *if* we had it. Rather we are proposing that the rudiments of a covenant ontology are already implicitly present in our best therapeutic work, and that what is already present in the practice of psychotherapy needs to be explicated as a more deliberate theory. Although we have employed the term *secular* psychotherapy, merely to underscore the fact that a truly efficacious healing process is at work without any deliberate religious ideology, we would much prefer (risking tautology) to speak only of a *so-called* " secular " psychotherapy, in order to point to the deceptive and illusory character of the whole concept of the secular, viewed from the deeper perspective of a covenant ontology.[34]

The following table will summarize the analogical relationships we have discussed as they apply to the cognitive, ontic, emotive, volitional, and relational dimensions of the self's functioning:

	THERAPIST'S ACTIVITY	HEALING PROCESS	CHRIST EVENT	BELIEVER'S RESPONSE
Understanding (Cognitive)	Empathetic understanding	Self-understanding	Humanity of God	Being known
Existing (Ontic)	Congruence	Self-identity	Deity of God	Being oneself
Feeling (Emotive)	Acceptance	Self-acceptance	Forgiveness of God	Being forgiven
Willing (Volitional)	Permissiveness	Self-direction	Grace of God	Being liberated
Acting (Relational)	Unconditional positive regard	Freedom for others	Love of God	Loving others

The healing process involves a fivefold development which may be seen as analogous to five aspects of the activity of God as celebrated in Christian worship and proclamation, corresponding also to five basic dimensions of a phenomenology of human existence (knowing, being, feeling, deciding, and doing), as follows: (a) The response of faith to the proclamation that God enters and shares the human frame of reference in his incarnate Word is the awareness that one is known and understood by the divine reality. Similarly, the healing process is initiated by the empathetic presence of the counselor in the frame of reference of the troubled person, enabling him to achieve an increasingly clear self-understanding in response to the experience of being understood by a human brother.

(b) The proclamation that God does not cease to be himself as he enters the human frame of reference, but that he remains wholly at one with himself, moves the faithful community to celebrate the congruence of the triune God in encountering human estrangement. Likewise, the analogy of faith sees the congruent therapist participating in the neighbor's estrangement without losing his identity, remaining fully open to his own immediate feelings in a way that frees the individual to move toward increased openness to himself and sharper self-identity. (c) The response of faith to the forgiveness of God is the experience of being accepted and received in spite of one's inadequacies. Similarly, as the therapeutic process proceeds, the individual experiences an increasing acceptance of himself amid his inconsistencies and bizarre feelings, which is enabled by the counselor's genuine acceptance of them. (d) The response of faith to the context of divine grace celebrated in eucharistic existence is the awareness of that liberating freedom which permits and calls man to be who he is. Similarly, out of a renewed self-understanding and self-acceptance, the individual in therapy begins actively to test his capacity for self-direction, made possible only in a permissive therapeutic context. (e) The response of faith to the loving, serving, caring action of God is an increased capacity to love, serve, and care for others. Analogously, the psychotherapeutic process is not complete until the individual comes to move toward others with genuine interest in the need of his neighbor, a movement that is increasingly enabled by the unconditional positive regard of the therapist.

We have sought a new basis for the *rapprochement* of theology and therapy through the juxtaposition of the helping process and God's help, hoping to clarify the distinction between man's self-knowledge and the divine self-disclosure, and the limited forms of the analogy between them. Our proposal is that such a basis recognizes that *the psychotherapeutic process, although distinct from revelation, implicitly presupposes an ontological assumption* — Deus pro nobis — *which is made explicit in the Christian kerygma and clarified by faith's response to revelation, and it is therefore possible by means of the analogy of faith to perceive Christologically the so-called secular counseling situation as the arena of God's self-disclosure.* If the self is understood, by definition, as unavoidably standing in relation to the One who gives it life, then understanding of oneself must in some sense be an understanding of that ultimate reality which is the ground and source of selfhood. This does not mean that self-understanding is synonymous with the divine self-disclosure, since revelation differs from insight in that the initiative for it comes from another. But the Other who speaks in authentic insight is spoken of in the witness of the Christian community. Revelation is related to insight as speaking is to hearing, however inadequately the hearer may know of the nature of the reality speaking to him in his insight into himself.

CHAPTER III

THE THEOLOGY OF CARL ROGERS

If it is possible for therapists to project themselves phenomenologically into the frame of reference of clients, it is also possible for theologians to take a phenomenological view of the process of psychotherapy, i.e., to enter the unique frame of reference of therapeutic interaction, try to understand what is happening, look at it unjudgmentally, with an attempt to perceive the therapist's work as he himself perceives it. Our intention in this section is to try to understand the inner reality of client-centered therapy purely from within its own frame of reference, and in the process to indicate how this procedure embodies a certain implicit theological orientation, which we hope to clarify.

If we mean by *theology* a deliberate and systematic attempt to speak self-consistently of man's predicament, redemption, and authenticity, then the therapeutic work of Carl Rogers has deep theological concerns, even though he has little to say formally about God. Our task in this section is not merely to suggest how Rogers' psychology can be translated into theological jargon, but to show that Rogers is *already* a theologian of sorts, and that it is not alien to his deeper intention to view his entire work as a kind of demythologized (or perhaps dekerygmatized) theology.

Although there may be many possible perspectives through which Rogers' theory of therapy might be meaningfully viewed, we believe that it lends itself quite naturally to phenomenological analysis under a *threefold structure* familiar to systematic theology, which begins with (*a*) an analysis of man's predicament, proceeds to (*b*) a discussion of the redemptive possibilities for deliverance from that predicament, and concludes with (*c*) a prospectus for the growth of the self toward maturity and self-fulfillment in response to this redemptive possibility.[1] We believe that Rogers' therapy can be understood quite easily, without forced exegesis, in terms of this threefold structure of sin, grace, and authenticity.

Mark carefully that, far from merely applying theological *terms* as an overlay to Rogers' concepts, we are, rather, asserting that he is already a theologian of considerable strength, whether or not he would wish to admit it. Neither are we speaking merely of *analogies* to a theology of man, reconciliation and sanctification, but of a constructive Rogerian *credo* that includes a rather thoroughgoing analysis of man as a gifted and fallen creature (a systematic anthropology), a presentation of a new possibility for self-fulfillment given in a saving event (a systematic soteriology), and finally a prospectus on the growth of the self toward self-acceptance, full functioning and authenticity (a systematic ethic and doctrine of sanctification).

Although there are many passages in Rogers' writing where this implicit theological perspective becomes apparent, we will specify three particular essays that illustrate its structure most clearly: " A Theory of Therapy, Personality and Interpersonal Relationships, as Developed in the Client-centered Framework,"[2] " Toward a Modern Approach to Values: The Valuing Process in the Mature Person,"[3] and " A Process Conception of Psychotherapy."[4]

These are the best guides to the three major themes of Rogers' theology.

Before we proceed into theological analysis, it is significant to note that the therapist who has perhaps contributed most to contemporary pastoral care and, it can be argued, has contributed as much as any other living man to current psychotherapy, was at one time vocationally committed to the Christian *ministry*. Although we would not want to argue that Rogers' therapy is derived basically or unilaterally from the Christian tradition, there is undoubtedly a deep subsoil of Christian devotion underneath his entire empathetic orientation, which cannot be ignored if one looks seriously at the direction of his whole career of vocational service. Rogers was deeply involved in the student Christian movement during his university years at Wisconsin, where after first studying agriculture, he then decided to enter the Christian ministry. In fact, so deeply was he involved in the student movement that he was delegated to go to China for a World Student Christian Federation conference in 1922. So a profound Christian heritage was already at work as leaven amid his personal history long before he took up his work as a psychotherapist. Attending Union Theological Seminary in 1924, he met a group of students who wanted to explore some of their own supposedly "nontheological" questions and interests, and who, like many theologues today finally "thought themselves right out of religious work."[5] They perceived a deeper-than-churchly ministry through involvement in the secular processes of healing. In his autobiography, Rogers insists that he moved out of religion into psychology in order to gain freedom *from* religious doctrines, in order that he could explore his own questions. As Rogers relates his own personal history, however, it becomes clear that his emancipation from the narrow bounds of a "highly conservative and almost fundamentalist Protestant Christianity"[6] was an appropriate and maturing rejection of an arbitrary, oppressive, heteronomous religious authority, and a movement toward autonomy, freedom, and self-discovery, which is not at all inimical to the core of the Protestant tradition.

Since Rogers himself applies his theory of therapy to *all* interpersonal relationships, and invites others to do so, we believe that it is not at all foreign to his basic orientation to attempt to correlate the therapeutic process with a theology of revelation. Rogers himself insists that his experience as a therapist has led him "to formulate theoretical statements regarding *all* interpersonal relationships, seeing the therapeutic relationship simply as one special case."[7] He further argues that if his views of therapy have any validity at all, they will lend themselves to "application in all those fields of human experience and endeavor which involve (*a*) interpersonal relationships and (*b*) the aim or potentiality of development or change in personality and behavior."[8] Whatever one might think of theology, it is clear that both of these fields are focal theological concerns. So Rogers is, in a way, inviting us to correlate client-centered therapy with wider interdisciplinary insights, a task toward which little has been seriously contributed to date by the mainstream of Protestant theology.

At times Rogers argues quite explicitly that "truth is unitary," only to add, "even though we will never be able to know this unity."[9] He does assert his faith, however, that "a complete theory of the individual plant would show us 'what God and man is.'"[10] Thus, if any process is known with full adequacy, such knowledge can be extended to other forms of knowledge.

Rogers insists that whatever he has discovered about therapy has merely been perceived as an "orderliness which was inherent in the experience."[11] The essential hu-

mility of his approach to science is apparent in his declaration that "though there may be such a thing as objective
truth, I can never know it; all I can know is that some
statements appear to me subjectively to have the qualifica-
cations of objective truth. Thus there is no such thing as
Scientific Knowledge; there are only individual perceptions of what appears to each person to be such knowledge." [12]

One of Rogers' most impressive philosophical constructs,
to this writer, is his principle that "*what is most personal
is most general.*" [13] If one can understand what is most real
within his own experience and unique for oneself at the
deepest personal level of feeling and understanding, it is
likely that it is "the very element which would, if it were
shared or expressed, speak most deeply to others." [14] It is
because this writer has so personally experienced both the
process of client-centered therapy and the liberating
Word of the Christian kerygma, and yearned for them to
be related, that this whole enterprise has been undertaken,
in the hope that others who have shared some of these
same intuitions would wish to have them set forth for systematic consideration. It is in this spirit that we proceed
to speak of the theology of Carl Rogers.

1. Sin

We will discuss the first major phase of Rogers' theology,
the doctrine of man's estrangement from himself, in three
stages: (a) man's original condition and possibility;
(b) the fall, and (c) the bondage of the will. A more
Rogerian vocabulary would speak of these factors as:
(a) the self-actualizing tendency; (b) incongruence; and
(c) distortion in awareness, defense, and anxiety.

a. Man's original condition and possibility. A clue to the
subtle depth of Rogers' entire theology is the way in which

he dialectically combines a very high doctrine of the original possibility of man (*imago Dei*) with an equally high doctrine of man's wretched fallenness and estrangement from himself. It can be easily shown that this dialectic does not differ in its basic structure from the Pauline-Augustinian-Protestant dialectic of the estranged creature, created for authentic life in the image of God, yet existing in a wretched estrangement from himself, a cleavage which prevents him from fully being himself.[15] In both perspectives, the hiatus within the self cannot be bridged through one's own initiative from within the framework of one's own inauthenticity. Because of various stratagems of self-deception, which keep the self imprisoned in its own estrangement, the estranged man has *lost* his potentiality for fulfillment and stands in desperate need of some new redemptive power to enable reconciliation to himself.

Although the Christian tradition views this estrangement as a universal human condition which demands a divine act for its resolution, whereas Rogers' view does not clearly specify either its inevitability or the necessity of an *opus Dei* for its cure, nevertheless we wish to show that the essential dialectic of the Christian doctrine of the estrangement of man's created nature is deeply embedded in Rogers' theory of therapy. However much he may insist upon the human possibility for growth and insight under the appropriate conditions, Rogers does not dilute in the slightest the depth character of the human predicament. To clarify the two sides of this dialectic — both the original possibility of man for authenticity and the estranged condition of the incongruent man — is now our task.

The human *infant,* as described by Rogers in his essay on value theory, prefers from the outset those experiences which maintain and enhance his total organism. The neonate experiences a flexible *organismic valuing process* wherein the locus of valuation is within the organism, not introjected from the outside. Unlike most of us, the infant typically knows what he likes and dislikes.[16] Healthy organismic valuing, and thus healthy psychological functioning, may be observed in the newborn child "who at one moment values food, and when satiated, is disgusted with it; at one moment values stimulation, and soon after values only rest; who finds satisfying that diet which in the long run most enhances his development." Rather like Bultmann's view of authentic intentionality, which affirms that the self is always searching for possibilities for self-fulfillment in whatever activity it pursues, even though the act may not be properly self-fulfilling, Rogers asserts an "inherent tendency of the organism to develop all its capacities in ways which serve to maintain or enhance the organism,"[17] even though this intention may be only seldom fulfilled.

To what extent does Rogers' view of man's *self-actualizing tendency* echo the Christian doctrine of the *imago Dei* and *justitia originalis?* The concept of the image of God alleges that man as creature is given the capacity to *mirror* or "image" the love of God in human relationships. Although this reflective capacity is always distorted under the conditions of estrangement (the mirror is *always* broken!), nevertheless the mirror is *intended* to function and is given to the natural man by the grace of the Creator for the purpose of being used. Although a broken mirror, it nevertheless inviolably remains a mirror of some kind, without which it is impossible to define man. A powerful strand of Christian anthropology argues that it is impossible to take away from man this capacity to image God. However distorted by sin, the original righteousness of man (*justitia originalis*) consists in the fact that once given, the mirror can never finally be eradicated from his humanity, however dully or brokenly it may reflect the divine glory. Although Rogers, of course, has no such view of man's primordial condition, or of the will of God as the end of authentic self-actualization, nevertheless his emphatic insistence upon the inviolability of the self-actualizing tendency can be viewed as a secularized way of speaking of the persistent impulse in man toward authenticity, in a way similar, despite differences, to the inviolability of the *imago Dei*.

b. The fall of man is described by Rogers in developmental categories: The infant, born with the capacity for organismic valuing, unfortunately (and we presume inevitably) learns from his environment certain introjected value constructs which are superimposed upon his own experience. The locus of evaluation shifts away from the experiencing organism. The self (to which we refer when we say "I" or "me") loses touch with its own concrete experiencing process, or symbolizes it poorly. The self grows increasingly alienated from its own feelings.[18] There develops a basic distrust in the growing child of his own experiencing process, and of himself as a process, since his experiences do not always coincide with these introjected values his parents and significant others say are good. Toilet training illustrates this. The child is asked to accept many abstract introjected value constructs which he does not himself personally experience and which are often widely divorced from his own range of symbolization and feeling. Thus as the organism develops in human society, or at least in modern Western cultures, the human self *falls* from organismic experiencing. One is forced to leave the Eden of the neonate situation in which valuing is deeply rooted in concrete experiencing and is cast out into the alien land of incongruence, in which there is a disjunction between selfhood and experience.

It is ordinarily only after many years of such alienation, when incongruence has deepened and crystallized, that the person may come to the psychotherapist for help to "find himself again." In early stages of therapy, the person ordinarily is trapped in a state of fixity and remoteness of experience. There is a severe blockage of internal communication. Constructs are rigid. Communication is only about externals, non-self items. Experiencing is structure bound. There is no desire to change.[19] Often the person entering therapy only hopes that it will reinforce presupposed personal constructs and introjected values, and often the most remote possibility imagined is that therapy might help them become free from these rigid constructs which are disrelated to their own experiencing process.

Rogers' view of the human predicament is summed up in the construct *incongruence*. When a discrepancy occurs between the way the self symbolizes itself and the actual experience of the organism, there exists a state of incongruence between self and experience.[20] If *self* is defined as " the organized, consistent conceptual gestalt composed of perceptions of the characteristics of the ' I ' or ' me,' " [21] and if *experience* means " all that is going on within the envelope of the organism at any given moment which is potentially available to awareness," [22] then incongruence is most compactly defined as a disjunction between self and experience.

Thus the human predicament centers in the fact that one cannot be himself, cannot feel his feelings, cannot symbolize his experience adequately, and therefore is estranged from himself. The Biblical *locus classicus* for such incongruence between self and experience is Rom., ch. 7, where Paul states that man is not able to do what he really wills. He is divided from himself. He cannot actualize his true intention. Rogers' unintentional but excellent exegesis of Rom., ch. 7, sounds like this: "Thus the neurotic behavior is incomprehensible to the individual himself, since it is at variance with what he consciously 'wants' to do, which is to actualize a self no longer congruent with experience." [23]

c. The bondage of the will. Like the Fourth Gospel, Tertullian, Augustine, Calvin, Kierkegaard, and many other theologians before him, Carl Rogers develops a clear, tough-minded statement of *the bondage of the will* as a central feature of the human quandary, according to which man in his fallen condition is not even aware of his fallenness. One of the hallmarks of man's predicament is that he is blind to the very existence and character of his predicament. The possibility he most fears is the thought of someone undermining his rigid, defensive personal constructs which separate him from himself. [24]

This revised version of the classical Christian doctrine *de servo arbitrio* is forcefully developed by Rogers' discussion of the dynamics of *distortion in awareness* and denial to awareness, a process by which "material which is significantly inconsistent with the concept of self cannot be directly and freely admitted to awareness." [25] Thus whenever experiences are subceived (discriminated without awareness) as incongruent with the self-structure, the organism responds by denying the experience to awareness.

The radical character of human bondage to inauthenticity is further developed in Rogers' discussion of the dynamics of *defense*, through which the self, in seeking to protect itself from self-disclosure and health (*salvus*), erects barriers to self-awareness whenever an experience is perceived as incongruent with the self. The goal of defensiveness is thus to maintain the fixed, current, recalcitrant inauthenticity of the self and not to admit the threatening new experience into consciousness.

Whereas health would consist of an organismic valuing process in which "experiences are being accurately symbolized and continually and freshly valued in terms of the satisfactions organismically experienced," [26] the predicament of man deepens as heteronomous introjected values force the indvidual to live in terms of certain *conditions of worth* which arise "when the positive regard of a significant other is conditional, when the individual feels that in some respects he is prized and in others not." [27] He learns that his existence is valued by others only conditionally, and thus in classical theological language he is only justified by works, by something that he can do to fulfill these conditions of acceptance. He can value himself only insofar as he fulfills these expectations of others which will make him feel valued and valuable. So his life increasingly becomes an attempt to climb the ladder of self-justification, buying acceptance and affirmation from others by fulfilling their conditions of worth.

The self-defeating character of this bondage of the will is seen in the increased loss of touch with one's own organismic valuing process, as the dynamics of incongruence, distortion in awareness, defense, and conditions of worth proceed. A major obstacle to self-awareness under such conditions is that there is no way of resolving contradictions among competing value constructs when they arise, since they are not testable, not subject to revision, but increasingly take on an absolutist character, not unlike the pharasaic legalism which was the subject of early Christian polemic.

Although often misinterpreted as an optimist who so insists on man's innate possibility for appropriate self-direction that he can see no genuine human predicament, Rogers himself says: " I would not want to be misunderstood on this. I do not have a Pollyanna view of human nature. I am quite aware that out of defensiveness and inner fear, individuals can and do behave in ways which are incredibly cruel, horribly destructive, immature, regressive, antisocial, hurtful." [28]

Rogers' hard line on the bondage of the will is finally exhibited in his penetrating definition of *anxiety* as the response of the organism to the subception that the discrepancy between experience and self might possibly enter awareness, thus forcing a change in the self-concept. When the organism subceives such a discrepancy as approaching consciousness, anxiety is felt.[29] It cues the organism to the fact that some change in the self-structure might be forced if these incongruencies ever enter awareness. Thus it is that the individual experiences the uneasiness of anxiety, the origin of which is understandably diffuse and vague to the incongruent self. Thus anxiety perpetuates and elaborates the servitude of the will to incongruence.

If *sin* (*hamartia* in the New Testament) means missing the mark of one's authentic self,[30] then surely Rogers' analysis of the dynamics of incongruence constitutes a rich explication and fresh restatement of the doctrine of sin. Absent, of course, is the broader Christian interpretation which argues that man's self-estrangement is more deeply interpreted as estrangement from the ground of his being. Although Rogers says little along these lines, his analysis of the human predicament does not preclude such an elaboration, and in fact it can be argued, invites such an analysis. Of course, Rogers, for good reasons eschews such terms as sin, which lend themselves to a moralistic dilution of the human predicament, but the depth dimension of the human quandary is not thereby diminished in his theory of therapy.

2. REDEMPTION

Having clarified Rogers' profound analysis of the human predicament, we come now to ask how the estranged incongruent man is delivered from this predicament. Given the condition of self-alienation, how does it happen that a new relationship emerges as a saving event? Granted the wretched dynamics of the bondage of the will which prevent man from becoming aware of himself, what constitutes the new possibility for self-awareness, self-fulfillment, self-acceptance, and the reconciliation of man to himself?

For Rogers, *the saving event is the mediation of unconditional positive regard through a congruent and empathetic person.*[31] As the incongruent individual senses that he is prized and valued by another person who is at one with himself, who enters his internal frame of reference with understanding positive regard, he is freed to begin to value himself positively, become aware of his lost self, experience himself more fully, and be himself more completely.

How does one proceed to mediate this saving event and relationship? Rogers describes it in this way: " I would like him to know that I stand with him in his tight, constricted little world, and that I can look upon it relatively unafraid. . . . I would like to go with him on the fearful journey into himself into the buried fear, and hate, and love which he has never been able to let flow in him." [32] The mediator of the saving event thus engages in a certain kind of descent into hell, the hell of the internal conflict of the estranged man, a kenosis, an incarnate participation in the suffering of his human brother. Although he realizes that at times he may be perceived as an intruder

and a threat, he is willing to take that risk, to become all
things to all men in order that some shall be brought
again to health (*salvus*).[33]

It is truly illuminating to analyze theologically what is
meant by *unconditional positive regard*. In Rogers' own
language: " It involves the therapist's genuine willingness
for the client to be whatever feeling is going on in him at
that moment — fear, confusion, pain, pride, anger, hatred,
love, courage, or awe. It means that the therapist cares for
the client, in a non-possessive way. It means that he prizes
the client in a total rather than a conditional way." [34] It is
a " warm, positive and acceptant attitude toward what *is* in
the client." [35] In more precise formulation, " To perceive
oneself as receiving unconditional positive regard is to perceive that of one's self-experiences none can be discriminated by the other individual as more or less worthy of
positive regard." [36]

The analogy of faith reads this process under the illumination of the kerygma's explicit proclamation of the unconditional *agapē* of God, viewing the therapeutic process
from the vantage point of the divine redemptive process.
Although Rogers had nothing to say of the *amor Dei* as
the proper basis of understanding unconditional positive
regard, we have already shown that any effective therapy
is inevitably going to rely upon it, in an implicit sense.
Whether one buys that argument or not, however, it is
clear that, according to Rogers, no deliverance from bondage occurs without the unconditional positive regard of a
human brother.

We shall now delineate in greater detail the dynamics of
the saving event and relationship which, according to Rogers, enables human renewal and reconciliation. Assuming
that two persons are in psychological *contact* (they have
the minimum essential of a relationship, " when each

makes a perceived or subceived difference in the experiential field of the other "),[37] the conditions for deliverance from human bondage are as follows: (a) *When* one person exists in a state of incongruence, being vulnerable or anxious, and (b) another congruent person meets him with unconditional positive regard, entering into his frame of reference with empathetic understanding, and (c) when the troubled individual perceives himself as recipient of this unconditional positive regard and empathetic understanding, (d) *then* growth toward fuller human functioning occurs, the syndrome of bondage is broken, the self is offered the possibility of renewal and self-reconciliation.[38] In a moment of bold confidence in the efficacy of this saving relationship, Rogers goes so far as to argue that when these conditions are present, "constructive personal development will *invariably* occur."[39]

Thus at the center of Rogers' theology stands a strong soteriology (doctrine of salvation), which argues that when certain conditions are present, the resolution of the human predicament occurs, or at least can occur. Therapy does not consist in the proclamation of these conditions, but of the concrete mediation of them through a relationship that frees the self to be itself. Rogers' view is sometimes called "relationship therapy" since its basic hypothesis is that there is a certain type of relationship through which troubled persons discover within themselves "the capacity to use that relationship for growth."[40] In this relationship the reality of acceptance must be made transparently real to the anxious and defensive individual. Only when the congruent neighbor can dwell for a time in the private world of the fragmented man without judgment or evaluation, mediating an attitude of warmth, interest, respect, care, concern, and understanding, unconditionally prizing each fluctuating facet of the individual's self-ex-

pression and consciousness as it reveals itself, only then is
the demonic power of human estrangement broken. Only
when the therapist believably mediates the reality of acceptance grounded in being itself is healing *possible* and
therefore from time to time *actualized*.

Unconditional positive regard is directed not only toward the individual as he is but also toward his whole potentiality to become an authentic person with full humanity. Rogers quotes with approval Buber's statement that
true dialogue involves affirming the other as he is created
to become, positively regarding his whole future uniquely
personal *potentiality*, not merely his present broken actuality, although his present brokenness admittedly must be
received also in unconditional acceptance.[41] Nothing else
saves. Not technique, not expertise, not diagnosis, not
medications, not incisive analysis — none of these suffice
to free the individual from the particular bondage of the
will of which we have spoken; only the unconditional positive regard of a congruent empathetic neighbor.

Thus client-centered therapy is not a technique or some
vastly improved " non-directive method " [42] by which we
have learned secretly to manipulate people toward goals
and constructive ideals which we envision as a better fulfillment of their humanity. Instead the effective counselor
must embody an attitude of unconditional affirmation and
acceptance, liberating love and concern rooted in reality
itself, genuinely valuing the person without conditions of
worth. Although very easy to state and buy as a cheap
abstract formula, this saving relationship is extremely rare
in an acquisitive society where everything is already
geared to presupposed conditions of worth, manipulation,
and depersonalization. How little help it is for the incongruent neighbor whose counselor may give platitudinous
lip service to the *ideas* of love and " the dignity of man," if

in subtle ways perhaps even unknown to himself he depersonalizes and disvalues the very person who exists concretely before him. If, on the other hand, this troubled man can genuinely feel himself within the context of unconditional positive regard in the presence of a congruent neighbor, free to explore the inconsistencies within himself, there are powerful healing vitalities in covenant creation itself which will then move him toward appropriate self-direction and the constructive resolution of inner conflict.

We have spoken of the saving *event* in the sense of a series of interpersonal occurrences, which enables human renewal. Note that the saving event or relationship that liberates the enslaved man is never merely the *idea* of an accepting reality or the neatly boxed abstract *notion* of positive regard, but the actual *mediation* of unconditional positive regard through a concrete interpersonal relationship! Likewise, in any vital soteriology the saving event will be more than an idea in our minds. The construct itself will exist as a response to a living relationship through which something new, some live possibility for self-understanding is offered which makes all things new.

Of course such a saving event, as Rogers explicates it, is not limited to formal psychotherapy with a trained counselor. Congruent understanding and unconditional positive regard can quite possibly be mediated in relationships between neighbor and neighbor, parent and child, teacher and student, lover and beloved, friend and friend. We can expect trained therapists to be better prepared to offer this healing relationship. Pastors, counselors, and others in the helping professions also ought to be more adept than others at engendering these conditions of personal growth. But whenever and wherever it occurs, in whatever institutional or noninstitutional context, whether in religious con-

fessional or over a coffee cup, whether on the couch of a
trained analyst or in a friendly chat with a fellow em-
ployee, anytime one incongruent human being finds himself in the presence of another who is congruent, who enters his frame of reference with empathetic unconditional
positive regard, when he perceives this, he is freed to discover himself more deeply and bring himself into better
touch with his concrete experience.[43] This is what happens in therapy, wherever it occurs.

The mystery, and the profoundly religious character of
the whole therapeutic process, is occasionally articulated
by Rogers: "I rejoice at the privilege of being a midwife
to a new personality — as I stand by with awe at the emer-
gence of a self, a person, as I see a birth process in which
I have had an important and facilitating part." [44]

One might object that since Rogers' view of the human
predicament lacks the distinctive Judeo-Christian element
of disobedience to God, and since his view of the saving
event lacks language about God's saving deed, there is little need even to compare them, much less to leave the implication that they are almost alike. Admittedly, while
pointing out the similarities, which we believe to be important, we must also indicate clearly that the saving
event in client-centered therapy is not to be uncritically
equated with the saving action of God in Jesus Christ,
however true it may be that they both mediate unconditional positive regard of an empathetic congruent neighbor. We have already spoken of the analogy and its limitations. Our purpose in this section is merely to enter
phenomenologically into the frame of reference of psychotherapy and attempt to clarify its implicit theological
self-understanding, showing how these processes are understandable within the framework of the classical categories of Protestant theology.

Although Rogers' view of the human predicament may be roughly described as having a " theological " character, it might be more seriously questioned as to whether his discussion of redemption is in any sense *theological,* properly speaking, since it does not speak of God at all, but only of human relationships. In reply, we return to our previous argument that these supposedly humanistic, horizontal, interpersonal relationships are the incognito of the reconciling God. Later in our discussion of Bonhoeffer,[45] we shall reject the whole notion of " two sphere " thinking, which easily separates the spheres of grace and nature, God and man, revelation and history, which are united in Jesus Christ.

Admittedly Rogers does not speak overtly about *God* in traditional theological categories. If he had, this chapter might not need to be written. Rogers himself has welcomed attempts to modify, elaborate, and complete his theoretical constructs by bringing further experiences to bear upon them. This is our intention as we have tried to speak of Rogers' therapy as a secularized doctrine of redemption. A principal gap in his theory of therapy, however, is the absence of any attempt to explicate the ontological basis of psychotherapy, upon which we believe the whole process to be dependent — the cosmic accepting reality that is witnessed to explicitly in the kerygma.

3. Authenticity

The final phase of Rogerian theology focuses upon man's growth toward self-fulfillment in response to unconditional positive regard and congruent empathy. How does the individual lay hold of the saving event so as to grow toward authenticity and self-actualization? If sanctification traditionally has meant the process of growth in grace toward true humanity, then we might inquire whether

Rogers has developed not only a doctrine of sin and redemption, but also of sanctification. Surprising as it may sound to ears trained to hear only secular sounds, we wish to argue that Rogers actually constructs rather precise dekerygmatized concepts of repentance, conversion, regeneration, growth in grace, sanctification, and perfection. The whole *ordo salutis* of classical Christian theology is thus recapitulated in secular language in Rogers' theory of therapy.

The heart of Rogers' doctrine of man's appropriation of the saving event is as follows: In response to empathetic positive regard, the individual increasingly is freed to admit incongruities to awareness, feel his feelings, and reorganize his self-concepts to include experiences that have been distorted and denied to awareness. " As this reorganization of the self-structure continues, his concept of self becomes increasingly congruent with his experience; the self now including experiences which previously would have been too threatening to be in awareness." [46] Thus in response to the saving event of unconditional positive regard the individual becomes increasingly able to value himself positively; in response to acceptance he is freed to accept himself; in response to the congruent other he moves toward congruence.

The process of growth toward authenticity is described by Rogers in a clear pattern of seven stages: (*a*) The earliest stage at the beginning of therapy is one of incongruence, blockage of internal communication, and self-alienation.[47] (*b*) As the person begins to experience empathetic positive regard, his feelings and expressions begin to flow, although expression is limited to non-self topics toward which he senses no personal responsibility. Although most feelings are still unowned, there is nevertheless some loosening in expression. (*c*) In due time this leads to a freer flow of speech related to one's self. Although experience is described mostly in the past tense, there is an increased loosening of symbolic expression, differentiation of feeling, and a dawning awareness of internal inconsistencies in one's self-concept.[48] (d) Finally, feelings begin to find expression in the present tense. Although there is still strong distrust of the process of self-disclosure, there is nevertheless an increasing exactness of expression and some desire to take responsibility for oneself. (e) In the fifth stage feelings are expressed more freely as in the present, are being more fully experienced with increased ownership. There is consequently a reduced blockage of internal communication and an increased facing of inconsistencies within the self. (f) At last personal growth takes on a real "process" quality. Symbolization is sharply improved. There is an increased immediacy of present experiencing and acceptance of feelings. (g) In the seventh and final stage, when therapy is ready to be terminated, there exists a continued and growing sense of ownership of fluxing feelings and a basic trust of one's own organismic valuing process. New feelings are experienced with full immediacy. Experience has lost most of its structure-bound aspects and becomes what Rogers calls "process-experiencing."[49] These are the basic stages of the process of growth toward authenticity and self-actualization, which corresponds to the classical theological construct of sanctification.

In traditional theological categories, the goal of sanctification is *perfection*. The process of growth aims at a full, totally adequate functioning, a complete embodiment of true humanity. Likewise the climax of Rogers' theology is his doctrine of the *fully functioning person,* a total processive response to the reality of acceptance, a total openness to experience, a full embodiment of mature self-actualization. The Eastern Orthodox tradition's conception of teleiosis (perfection) [50] as a process rather than a state is more compatible with Rogerian thought than the more rigid, static perfectionism of much Western spirituality. Any full functioning envisaged by Rogers would certainly involve an ongoing processive organismic development, ever changing with new circumstances, which would call for ever-renewed openness to oneself and sensitivity to one's environment. Rogers describes the fully functioning person as one who is fully alive in each moment, free to drop his facades, to trust his own organism, and to move toward self-direction, toward " being process, being complexity." [51] Or to put the whole process in a " crude equation ": " The more that the client perceives the therapist as real or genuine, as empathetic, as having an unconditional regard for him, the more the client will move away from a static, fixed, unfeeling, impersonal type of functioning, and the more he will move toward a way of functioning marked by a fluid, changing, acceptant experiencing of differentiated personal feelings. The consequence of this movement is an alternation in personality and behavior in the direction of psychic health and maturity and more realistic relationships to self, others, and the environment." [52]

He describes the valuing of the mature person as much like the infant, yet in some ways quite different. It is fluid, flexible, based on this particular moment, continually changing. The locus of evaluation is firmly established within the person as it had been within the neonate. He listens to himself. " He thrives on a maximum feedback interchange and thus, like the gyroscopic compass on a ship, can continually correct his course toward his true goal of self-fulfillment." [53]

Thus Rogers' description of sanctification involves a

process of *becoming who one is,* dropping phony roles and masks, experiencing oneself fully, and above all trusting one's own organismic valuing process, like the neonate. Echoing the injunction of Jesus, "Truly, I say to you, whoever does not receive the kingdom of God like a child shall not enter it" (Luke 18:17), Rogers' theology goes the full circle, just as traditional Christian theology does, from the original situation of man as open to himself, the fall of man into incongruence, the saving event of unconditional positive regard, and the growth of man toward a full functioning which is similar to the original situation of man prior to the fall.

Rogers further observes that in his dealing with clients there have been certain consistent *value directions* that appear with regularity, and with remarkable similarity, among widely varied clients. The most evident preference is for being real, being oneself, feeling one's own feelings. But equally important is a growing process of valuing others, being sensitive, appreciative of others just for what they are.

Persons who truly experience this delivering relationship, according to Rogers' observation, do not elect forms of antisocial behavior, such as fraud, murder, or dishonesty. The cause of such unfulfilling behavior is undermined by effective therapy. In his observation, persons who respond to unconditional positive regard are increasingly able to affirm and care for others out of the wealth of their own self-affirmation. "I believe that when the human being is inwardly free to choose whatever he deeply values, he tends to value those objects, experiences, and goals which make for his own survival, growth and development, and for the survival and development of others." [54] This *credo* is the central cornerstone of what might be called a Rogerian *ethic,* an understanding of the valuing process which emerges when one is truly being himself.

Whereas the Christian ethic of freedom, as articulated by Augustine, is a calling to love God and do as one pleases, since one who is constrained by the love of God is indeed free to serve the neighbor, likewise the therapeutic ethic of freedom, as articulated by Rogers, is a calling to understand oneself, trust one's own organismic valuing process, and in that sense follow one's deepest intention, since one who is in deepest contact with his own feelings is going to want to love, serve, and value others.

In the analysis of the self, Christian theology knows and has frequently spoken of three selves or three phases or conditions of the self which need to be distinguished: (a) the created self with its original potentialities (b) the fallen self with its distortions and incongruence, and (c) the redeemed self, the new man reconciled to the ground of his being and to himself. Although they are not clearly distinguished by Rogers, he nevertheless implicitly delineates these three stages of selfhood. When he speaks of trusting one's own organism, he is referring to the first and third stages, in which the self is free to trust its deepest, most authentic impulses and feelings. He is not referring to the fallen self, which is so estranged from itself that it can only follow spurious self-deceptive voices within itself which only lead it further into inauthenticity and bondage. Rogers is not suggesting that the individual can or should trust his own twisted feelings, since he cannot even fully feel them. Such talk applies only to the man who is growing out of self-alienation toward a capacity to contact his authentic feelings.

If it emerges in therapy, for example, that a person feels that he wants to be a thief, is the client-centered therapist called upon to help him to become a thief — to become who he is? Is this not the logic of self-direction, the cornerstone upon which client-centered therapy proceeds? Rogers seems to answer that no person, when he knows himself properly, actually wants to be a thief. The person who supposedly wants to be a thief is really aiming toward some kind of more legitimate, socially acceptable fulfill-ment. If he wants to be a thief at one stage of therapy, it remains the *faith* of the therapist, based upon long obser-vation and experience, that if the person is placed in a con-text in which he can truly understand himself, he will emerge with a capacity for social creativity and produc-tivity and will lay aside this temporary inauthentic will which is not his deepest intention. Does this mean that the therapist decides what his deepest intention is, thus an-nulling the central hypothesis of client-centered therapy? No. Therapy continues to proceed on the basis of a stub-born faith that the individual will direct himself appropri-ately if given an adequate context for self-understanding, but this faith has to be revalidated with every client. How can it be proved that this faith actually is reliable? There is no proof. The central hypothesis has to be tried again and again in every new therapeutic relationship.[55] Every client offers a new challenge for rediscovering or disprov-ing it. As faith, it is purely experimental, and one would hardly be inclined to believe it merely through rational persuasion. One must see it operating repeatedly in con-crete relationships before it is really credible. So the thera-pist does not try to help the person who wants to become a thief to become a good thief, but instead he tries to help him understand himself as one who at this point wants to be a thief. In effect he says, "We will explore your desire to be a thief. I have a hunch, if my experience with you is like others, that you will want to go beyond this on your own initiative, and that you yourself will choose yourself as something other than a thief." This hypothesis, which must be constantly reexamined with each new client, has much of the character of what traditional theology has called *faith*.

By authenticity we mean the process or condition of embodying and reflecting authentic or true humanity. Not only an explicit understanding of true humanity emerges in Rogerian theory, but also a definite way to actualize it is prescribed. Rogers is not content with merely developing a theory of psychotherapy, but he is equally concerned to spell out its relevance for interpersonal relationships, family life, education, group learning, etc.[56] Just as it is *from* his central therapeutic insight that he draws these wider conclusions ranging *to* the whole of human personal and social existence, likewise in Christian theology it is *from* its soteriological center that the Christian community has learned to think properly toward the circumference of human problems and relationships. As Rogers reasons from therapeutic empathy *forward* to the process of self-actualization, *backward* to an understanding of human estrangement, likewise Christian theology reads both consummation and creation from the event of redemption (cf. Colossians, Ephesians, Irenaeus, Augustine, Calvin, etc.). It is from the unique perspective of the alleged cosmic therapeutic event, the event of the healing of history, that Christian worship and proclamation looks both to the beginning and to the end of time. Rogers' single-minded insistence upon deriving conclusions about man's predicament and promise strictly from his experience as a therapist is curiously similar to Barth's single-minded determination to deal with both creation and eschatology from an exclusively Christological point of reference. If Barth is determined to know nothing except Jesus Christ and his relevance for human self-understanding, Rogers is equally determined to know nothing except the therapeutic process and its relevance for human self-understanding.

4. CONCLUDING CRITIQUE

The following table clarifies, in sum, the basic categories with which we have been dealing:

CLASSICAL THEOLOGICAL CONSTRUCTS	ROGERIAN CONSTRUCTS
The Human Predicament (Sin)	Incongruence, Introjected values, Conditions of Worth
The Saving Event (Redemption)	Empathy, Congruence, Unconditional Positive Regard
Growth in Grace (Authenticity)	Openness to Experience, Congruence, the Fully Functioning Person

Having reviewed the three basic phases of Rogers' secular theology, we are now in a position to offer a critique from the vantage point of a more explicit, deliberate Protestant theology. However significant and perceptive may be Rogers' contributions to a systematic understanding of the human predicament, redemption, and authenticity, certain points need amendment and further elaboration.

a. Our principal critique, already mentioned but now requiring more precise formulation, is that Rogers has sought no ontological understanding of the total frame of reference of the therapeutic process. Interested chiefly in the internal frame of reference of the subject self, his empiricist intuitions warn him strongly against the danger of extrapolating his thesis in the direction of the larger question of being itself. It is our conviction, however, that if his therapeutic insight is understood and elaborated in its deepest dimension, it will necessarily move in the direction of ontology and will be seen as relevant not only for a theory of interpersonal relationships and behavioral change, but also for the inquiry into being itself. It is precisely at this point that Christian worship and proclamation relate most meaningfully to the therapeutic process.

Cast in the language of the historic Christian tradition, our initial criticism suggests that his view of redemption fails to place itself in the context of a larger understanding of creation, history, and consummation. There is no effort made to place this highly germinative therapeutic insight into a total, world-historical frame of reference, which the Biblical witness finds necessary in its proclamation of the saving event. The only saving deed of which the early Christian community speaks is that of a Christ who is "before all things, and in him all things hold together" (Col. 1:17). Whereas Christian proclamation speaks of the self-disclosure of the accepting reality in a total salvation history wherein the mystery of creation is laid bare, fully disclosed for all who have eyes to see, Rogers speaks only of the process of interpersonal self-disclosure based upon the limited acceptance of a finite brother, with no salvation history to undergird it.

If Christian theology centers in the kerygmatic announcement that God has once for all acted to reclaim his broken creation, Rogers' secular theology remains a dekerygmatized, secular affirmation of the human possibility for redemption, omitting any overt proclamation of any divine deed. In therapy there is no cosmic salvation event which forms the basis of one's knowledge of the ground of acceptance, as in Christian worship. The therapeutic process limits itself strictly to the assumption that some accepting reality is being mediated through a special interpersonal relationship, without braving the question of the source of acceptance as a fundamental question of being.

Consequently Rogers develops a soteriology without a

Christology, i.e., a view of the saving process without a historical event which once for all manifests and defines that saving process and gives the history of salvation a center in time and space. It is a humanistic soteriology without any acknowledged celebration of God's act, God's acceptance, God's unconditional positive regard. We are not suggesting that his psychotherapy is thus debilitated by a lack of language about God, but that it is precisely at the point of the vacuity of a limited humanism that a deeper Christian humanism can pick up the thread, affirming all that has been said about therapy, but completing it with the proclamation of the self-disclosure of God as the ontological basis of the whole process.

b. Rogers' theology is a restricted humanism, which in the last analysis is a kind of dehumanization that fails to see man in his deepest dimension as under God, and exaggerates the human capacity for ultimate self-fulfillment apart from God's own delivering activity. Three specific *qualifications* of our thesis need to be spelled out in order to avoid the misleading idea that Rogers' view is, in our judgment, fully adequate as a theology: (1) His concept of *man* as a gifted and estranged creature fails to perceive man in the profound dimension of his being created, claimed, and judged by God. (2) His doctrine of *redemption* is narrowly limited to personal self-reconciliation, and has little to say about reconciliation of society or a broader hope for the redemption of the cosmos. (3) His view of growth toward *authenticity* lacks a fuller perception of human wholeness illuminated by the divine wholeness, a deeper full-functioning enriched by God's own gracious functioning. Thus what we have called a " saving event " in Rogers' theology is, according to Christian wisdom, not a saving event at all in the fullest sense, if the ultimate redemption of human history is finally in God's hands.

c. Rogers' concept of *introjected values* tends toward *antinomianism,* i.e., toward a blanket rejection of legitimate means of social control, ignoring the validity of moral constructs and external demands in the growth of personal freedom toward a mature conscience and social responsibility. However perceptive may be his theory of value, it needs to be set in the context of the classical Protestant dialectic between *gospel and law,*[57] if its intention is to be preserved without collapsing social structures into individualistic anarchy. This threefold dialect affirms the law, or introjected values, as (1) the custodian of man, to restrain his destructive antisocial impulses, which flourish demonically under the conditions of estrangement. Admittedly the law plays a large part in the dynamics of estrangement itself, according to the New Testament, but law is needed for restraint, once given the recalcitrant character of the human predicament. (2) Secondly, the law drives man to despair of his own righteousness, and thus exists as *preparatio evangelica.* Likewise in therapy the attrition of living under the conditions of worth set by others drives one in the direction of becoming aware of the need for a healing relationship. Only the grinding judgment of the law (introjected values) and the wretched inconsistencies experienced under its power will drive one into the painful and yet liberating context of therapy. (3) Finally, the law remains as a factor in the fully functioning, mature Christian life to guide the new man toward increased responsibility to the neighbor. Likewise, in therapy many introjected values will remain as a guide to the congruent person, as a check to his own organismic valuing process, and as a reminder of the funded moral experience of society.

d. Although much is omitted in such an implicit theology, which one might reasonably expect to find in a more systematic treatment, one serious omission that deserves to be noted is the absence in Rogers' discussion of a doctrine of the *church*, or put differently, the neglect of any concept of authentic human community. The whole helping process is dealt with in a highly individualistic manner. The delivering relationship is essentially a private conversation, not a shared community of renewed persons. There is no thought of developing or discovering the larger interpersonal context of a fuller functioning community through which congruence and openness could be nourished. Traditional Christian wisdom seems to be more perceptive in insisting that if genuine healing is to take place in the estranged man, he stands in dire need of a nurturing, disciplining, supportive community which would mediate to him the means of grace by which to feed and enable his freedom to love and serve in the midst of human alienation. If there is any optimism in Rogers' interpretation of man, it is his assumption that the single individual who has once experienced the power of acceptance can fend for himself in an estranged world without a continuing community of confession, education, witness, and life together.

CHAPTER IV

BARTH'S DOCTRINE OF ANALOGY

Having clarified the implicit basis of psychotherapeutic acceptance as the explicit concern of Christian proclamation, and having now examined the incognito theological stance of Rogerian therapy, we are now ready to explore in greater detail a major facet of our proposal, viz., the proper use of the concept of analogy in the dialogue with psychotherapy. Since the method of analogy has been used somewhat uncritically in this dialogue to date, we shall ask whether Karl Barth's concept of the analogy of faith promises to provide a more constrained, deliberate, consistent procedure of analogical thinking more appropriate for this dialogue than the previous dubious attempts at natural analogies.

The word "analogy" comes from the Greek *analogia*, meaning proportion or correspondence.[1] In its broadest meaning, an analogy is merely a comparison based upon some recognized resemblance, a generalization about how two different things are similar. Since everyday language is cluttered with innumerable analogies, it is difficult to make of analogy a useful tool for discrete, clear theological discourse. We will ask how analogy should function, if at all, in this conversation with psychotherapy. How can it be protected from fanaticism and exaggeration, and what is its special promise and limitation?

Although Karl Barth has been viewed by such responsible American critics as David Roberts as an exponent of an extreme position in Protestant thought which has "tended to shut off instead of to facilitate collaboration" between theology and psychotherapy,[2] we shall take it as our purpose to show that Barth's doctrine of analogy provides a unique, mature, and fresh basis for dialogue with therapy in a way totally impossible for liberal Protestantism.

If forced to categorize our basic orientation, we would readily acknowledge that the general theological stance of our inquiry might be fittingly termed *post-Barthian* (far more than simply Barthian or neoorthodox), implying a broad affirmation of Barth's basic dogmatic achievement, yet with a determination to develop it in directions toward which Barth himself has never ventured. If Barth's contribution stands in the background as the precondition of our entire inquiry into psychotherapy, we would like to insist no less emphatically that we will proceed in the post-Barthian spirit of those such as Bonhoeffer, Hromádka, Stringfellow, Gollwitzer, and Ott,[3] all of whom share not only the rich bequest of Barth's achievement but also the determination to engage Barth in a worldly dialogue with contemporary secularity which he himself has never steadfastly pursued.

1. DEFINING AND LIMITING THE ANALOGY OF FAITH

a. The Definition of *Analogia Fidei.* Note carefully the unique analogical procedure suggested by Barth. The analogy of faith is defined most compactly as a relationship of correspondence (to be distinguished from parity and disparity) "in which human knowledge of God is converted into man's being known by God."[4] According to this analogy man only "knows by being known of God."[5] The term "analogy of faith" is taken from Rom. 12:6, *analogia tēs pisteōs*, which Barth exegetes as "the correspondence of the thing known with the knowing, of the object with the thought, of the Word of God with the word of man in thought and in speech."[6]

The analogy of faith views the natural entity or relationship under the illumination of God's self-disclosure. It proceeds strictly to ready the analogy *from* covenant *to* creation, from the action of God to human actions, from the Christ event to historical events. It reads the human relationship from the viewpoint of its being related to the self-disclosing God. It views human knowing from the vantage point of its being known by God.[7]

Far from claiming that our words, views, or concepts grasp God (as if he were our object to claim and control), Barth is arguing that God in his freedom claims us and our views, concepts, and words in such a way that it is only possible to speak of him in and through a genuine correspondence which he himself makes possible! "Our words are not our property, but His. And disposing of them as His property, He places them at our disposal — at the disposal of our grateful obedience — when he allows and commands us to make use of them in this relationship too."[8] So when we apply to God such human language as love, father, or lord, we are not alienating our language from its original intent, but restoring it to its deeper functional intent.

Barth defines the task of theology strictly as the self-examination of the Christian church with respect to the content of its distinctive utterance concerning God.[9] If dogmatics is "the self-test to which the Christian Church puts herself in respect of the content of her peculiar language about God,"[10] the whole theological enterprise must proceed on the basis of some sort of *correspondence* between God's word and our attempts to reflect it in human words. " Language about God has the proper content, when it conforms to the essence of the Church, i.e., to Jesus Christ . . . (Rom. 12:6). Dogmatics investigates Christian language by raising the question of this conformity. Thus it has not to discover the measure with which it measures, still less to invent it. With the Christian Church it regards and acknowledges it as given." [11]

How dare we use *our* frail, culturally shaped language to speak of God at all? " To the question how we come to know God by means of our thinking and language, we must give the answer that of ourselves we do not come to know Him, that, on the contrary, this happens only as the grace of the revelation of God comes to us and therefore to the means of our thinking and language, adopting us and them. . . . We are permitted to make use, and a successful use at that, of the means given to us." [12] If Christian faith speaks only of the living God who has made himself known, then it does not search for God, since it understands that it has already been discovered by the goal of its searching. Faith then proceeds to use human language to reflect analogically upon itself as having been known and discovered by God. Hence, the analogy of faith. Thus from time to time our own broken human language is " raised from the dead," [13] the death of its own pointing merely to created objects, and raised into the life of its being used to point to the One to whom it exists in response.

Although Barth is very cautious about employing analogy at all in theological reflection, and does so only under the strictest limitations, keenly aware of its dangers, he nevertheless feels compelled to do so on the basis of certain exegetical decisions, wherein Scripture continually

leads him to view the human situation under the analogy
of the divine activity. " If we are not disobedient but obedient to the truth of this revelation in taking up this particular word; if our decision for the concept of analogy is
not arbitrary; if it is not self-grounded upon a secret preju-
dice in favour of an immanent capacity of this concept,
but occurs under the compulsion of the object; if it is not,
then, a systematic but an exegetical decision, for this reason and to this extent it was and is a right decision." [14]
Barth also finds precedent for his doctrine of analogy in
Luther's maxim: *per fidem fit homo similis verbo Dei.*[15]

b. Illustrating the Analogy. The following examples will
serve to show the unique and deliberate procedure by
which Barth proposes to read the *analogia fidei* as a special method of knowing, a knowing oneself as having been
known.

(1) Barth's most frequent illustration of the analogy of
faith is *the correspondence between God's fatherhood and
human fatherhood.* Our word " father," he argues, derives
its first and final meaning not from the ordinary fact of human fatherhood, but in its correspondence to the action
of God, whom faith has learned to call Father. " No human father is the creator of his child, the controller of its
destiny, or its saviour from sin, guilt and death." [16] God
alone is properly and primarily *Father,* and faith knows
this by its being known as Son. " But it is of this Father's
grace that, in correspondence to his own, there should exist a human fatherhood also. . . . According to Eph. 3:15
God is the Father of whom the whole family (*pasa
patria*) in heaven and on earth is named. Hence in Is.
63:16 appeal is made to Him beyond all human fathers:
' Thou art our father, though Abraham be ignorant of us,
and Israel acknowledged us not: Thou, O Lord, art our
father.' Hence the warning of Jesus: ' And call no man

your father upon the earth: for one is your Father, which is in heaven' (Mt. 23:9)." [17] And yet human fatherhood is " set alongside the incomparable fatherhood of God, and human parents stand in the light of this analogy." [18]

(2) *Patience,* whether found in love, politics, psychotherapy, or parental conflict, is not finally understandable as a human virtue per se, but only in correspondence with " the incomprehensible being and attitude of God which is shown in the fact that he gives us time to believe in Him." [19] Thus human patience is most profoundly viewed under the analogy of the patience of God, which faith knows only in its being known by the patient God.

(3) Another example: When we speak of God as creator or *lord,* this *lordship* " is not first and properly what we know as the exercise of power by man over man, but the *kuriotēs* of God exercised and revealed in Jesus Christ." [20] Although admittedly most cultures and languages are acquainted with general ideas of lordship and creating and speak of other lords and creators than he who makes himself known in Jesus Christ, it is not good enough for Christian faith merely to *borrow* the general idea of lord and to expand it infinitely, only to claim that it has arrived at the same reality to which the church witnesses as the Lordship of God in Jesus Christ. Neither can we derive a genuine Christian understanding of *creation* merely by taking the general human notion of an artisan who creates something, and then projecting it to an infinite dimension, claiming this as the *Creator Spiritus* of Christian worship. For our ideas of lords and creators die with us. All *our ideas* must finally acknowledge another lordship, " a lordship even over our being in death, a genuinely effective lordship." Mark carefully: " If an analogy of God fails at this decisive point, if God Himself has to be added to give content and substance to what is supposed to be analogous

to Him, it is obviously useless as an analogy of God." [21]

(4) Likewise, in a final example crucial to our project: we cannot begin with human notions of *reconciliation* or redemption (as perhaps are knowable to psychotherapy) and, by infinitizing them, claim that we have come to know the God who reveals himself in Jesus Christ as reconciler and redeemer. If we know anything about God as reconciler, it is strictly because God has disclosed himself in a reconciling event and person, overturning all our petty notions of reconciliation, surprising all our limited expectations about what authentic redemption means! For our part we can only be grateful that God is reconciler and has made himself known as such. But any attempt to speak of God as reconciler on the basis of our previously defined ideas of reconciliation (whether borrowed from psychotherapy, drama, or jurisprudence) is in the last analysis to point not to God but to ourselves, to some merely hoped-for reconciliation which exists only in the sphere of our choice and definition. Any redemption that we can choose and define on our own initiative, we can also negate and redefine, and this would in no sense be God's own redemptive act!

Tillich has made considerable use of the general interpersonal idea of reconciliation in his theology, as a concept which can be read analogically toward Christology. " But when God makes peace with the world in His Son," Barth on the contrary argues, " He does something *very different* from completing what we with unbroken optimism find prepared in all nature and history, and in all the maturing experience of our life." [22]

" Where then is the analogy on the basis of which the knowledge of God is possible to us? " Barth asks. " If there is a real analogy between God and man — an analogy which is a true analogy of being on both sides, an analogy in and with which the knowledge of God will in fact be given — what other analogy can it be than the analogy of being which is posited and created by the work and action of God Himself, the analogy which has its actuality from God and from God alone, and therefore in faith and in faith alone?" [23] In sum: *We have no analogy of the being of God except that which is posited in his activity and which is therefore known only in faith,* if faith means response to God's self-disclosure. We cannot derive knowledge of God from already presupposed natural analogies, but " only in an analogy to be created by God's grace, the analogy of grace and faith to which we say Yes as the inaccessible which is made accessible to us in incomprehensible reality." [24]

A personal illustration may sharpen the focus of this analogical procedure. Recently I sat beside a glassy, still lake, the smooth surface reflecting the image of trees on the other side. I simply absorbed the beauty of the scene for a few deep, enriching moments. Then the thought struck me — Ah ha! It is true. Nature mirrors the beauty, glory, and majesty of God! So it seemed true at that moment. Then a bit of analogical reflection ensued. From the strict point of view of natural, empirical observation, what I am seeing is merely nature mirroring *nature,* not *God.* Only nature (trees, sky, color, light, etc.) is the visible partner. Yet my deeper impulse, unconsciously following the analogy of faith, was to read the natural object from the viewpoint of faith's confession of the Creator God. Faith can quite truly confess that nature mirrors God, because it does, but in so confessing we are grasping for human language to articulate our being grasped by God. We are perceiving in the natural object more than natural vision can modestly see with its empirical tools and vision. Only the eye of faith sees the analogy of faith, whereas the mirroring of nature is visible to the eye of rational-empirical analysis without faith.

Having framed this analogical procedure, Barth then surprisingly as ever proceeds to assert that even our very Western concept of analogy itself is only understandable and possible in the light of the analogy of faith! Even our "human word 'similarity' participates in the (as such) incomprehensible similarity which is posited in God's true revelation." [25] Our speech can only exist in response to God's own original speech in creation! Our speech thus inevitably participates in God's speaking and is constituted by a response to God's speech (cf. the later Heidegger who follows Barth formally on this point). This fact itself should call men to a continuing search for appropriate language that will reflect God's own speech in creation and reconciliation.

c. The Limitations of Analogical Thinking. Any analogy between the divine life and interpersonal processes is limited by the fact that it is always only a *partial correspondence.* "God is always God and man is always man in this relationship." [26] Whenever we attempt to speak of God in roughhewn human language, "each step that we take as we come from the hiddenness of God must, and will, consist in a new reception of the grace of revelation." [27]

For this reason the concept of analogy must be strictly distinguished from the concept of *parity* which asserts a simple synonymity between our language and God's being. For " what we are dealing with is *a similarity in spite of a greater dissimilarity.*" [28]

It is important to note that " only things which differ can be alike, and only like things differ." [29] One cannot speak of the incarnation and empathy as being analogous, e.g., *if* they are identical! Two synonymous concepts cannot be compared. Thus the very structure of analogy implies that

things must be different to be alike. So it is that God's unconditional acceptance and the positive regard of the empathetic human brother can be compared only because
they are different. So from the beginning there can be no
question of a simple *parity* or *univocity* in our discussion
of language about God and psychotherapy.

If analogy is not a simple *parity,* it also must be sharply
distinguished from a radical *disparity* which asserts that
God is in *no* way reflected by our limited categories and
imprecise language. Against both parity and disparity,
Barth defines *analogy* as a limited or partial similarity of
differing things.[30] Thus the concept of analogy of faith differs from (1) a *univocal* use of language which would allege that the word "father," e.g., has precisely the same
meaning when applied to God and to man (reducing the
analogy to simple parity), just as it differs from (2) an
equivocal use of language which would suggest that the
same word has utterly different meanings when applied
to God and to man (on the assumption that there is an
unbridgeable disparity between human language and
God's revelation).

2. CAN THE ANALOGY BE APPLIED TO THERAPY?

Granted that the *analogia fidei* may be generally useful
as a tool of theological epistemology, it remains to be seen
how it could apply to psychotherapy.

The roadway of the dialogue between theology and
therapy is strewn with numerous analogies. These attempts may be found, a dime a dozen, in most of the discussions of this subject that have been written during the
last forty years. Among the flood of attempts to develop
analogies between sin and neurosis, e.g., one might men-
tion those by Roberts, Hiltner, Tillich, Reinhold Niebuhr,
Elliott, and Mowrer.[31] Many others have tried to develop

analogies of one kind or another between therapy and redemption, salvation or justification (Williams, Tillich,
Hiltner, Van Deusen, Hulme, Kreutzer, to note a few).[32]
Dozens of more or less scholarly articles could be added to
the list of these discussions.[33] We have no lack of analogical reflection in this sphere. What we do lack, however, is
a constrained, careful use of analogy, deliberately conceived out of a clear, self-consistent theological method
and grounded in a serious doctrine of revelation. This has
not been achieved and has hardly been attempted.

Most previous analogical attempts have developed *natural analogies,* i.e., analogies that seek to derive theological conclusions from natural processes and relationships.
Under this procedure, one first examines a secular process
such as psychotherapy *as* an interpersonal relationship,
and only then reflects upon its theological significance. If
one begins with the secular process, *un*theologically understood, and only then moves from there to its implications for Christian doctrines of sin, grace, etc., one has already made crucial theological decisions, and from our
point of view conceded the most strategic battle before
the first shot was fired. The literature on theology and
therapy to date has exhibited an overwhelming confidence
that theological learnings can be derived from therapeutic
learnings, but often in the spirit of one picking up crumbs
from the master's table and deluding himself into believ-
ing it was a banquet.

Without totally denying the validity of all these efforts,
we intend to show that the analogy can and must be read
the other way, deriving psychotherapeutic learnings from
theological learnings, reading the process of human self-
disclosure from the vantage point of the divine self-disclosure, thinking through the therapeutic process from the
perspective of its being illuminated by the empathetic love

of God in Jesus Christ as the ontological basis for secular healing.[34] To utilize effectively Barth's concept of correspondence in rereading this analogy is now our task.

Barth himself does not attempt to apply the analogy of faith to the dialogue with psychotherapy. The five forms of analogy which we have spelled out in Chapter II already constitute a much more extensive discussion of this application than any of the slight hints which we might find in Barth's own writings. However, we can at least set forth a couple of examples which show that its application to psychotherapy is not completely foreign to his basic intention.

The first example is the correspondence between Barth's view of *honoring the neighbor* and the therapeutic concept of *unconditional positive regard*. Whereas Rogers urges us to value others positively, prizing them with unconditional acceptance, Barth deepens this whole attitude by calling upon us to honor and value other men because they have been honored and valued by God. The value which God accords to man is that he shares in human existence, honors humanity by becoming man. We are therefore free to accept this recognition and esteem of God, allowing ourselves to be honored by God, and honoring others as such.[35]

Here is the analogy of faith as applied to the question of unconditional positive regard: We are called to reflect the honor of God by honoring our neighbors, whether or not our neighbor is aware of his being honored by the Creator in his very creation. "Man does not cease to be man even when his whole environment and he himself cease to remember God and fall victim to the overlooking, forgetting, mistaking and falsifying of his honour as man. Hence the honor itself, precisely because it is not his but the reflection of the glory of God falling upon him, cannot be lost. It belongs to the *character indelebilis* of his human existence." In a more concise phrase, Barth declares, " Man can be godless, but God . . . does not become ' manless.' " " There is no ontological godlessness." [36]

A second example which strongly suggests the potential application of Barth's analogy to psychotherapy centers in his frequent statement that God only wishes us to *be ourselves*. As with Rogers, the goal of authentic life is truly to become oneself. The deepest ethical imperative, for both Barth and Rogers, is: *Werde wer du bist!* (Become who you are!) Since Barth understands the self under the analogy of faith, however, the self that we are called to become is understood basically (contra Rogers) as the self who has already been created, judged, and redeemed by God in Jesus Christ. The self *is* always already covenant partner with God, however much it may deny its authentic selfhood, and its task is to become itself in the fullest sense. Yet it is significant that Barth insists as emphatically as Rogers that " Man is summoned to be himself." [37] Although the self is variously defined by Barth and Rogers, the call to self-acceptance, self-affirmation, self-fulfillment, self-actualization remains formally the same. " ' Become what you are,' means therefore: ' Grow into your character, accept the outline of your particular form of life, the manner of existence which in your special struggle of the Spirit against the flesh will emerge more clearly as your own, as the one which is intended for you, as the form of the life alloted and lent to you by God." [38]

The whole demand for self-affirmation and self-actualization, however, is read under the *analogia fidei* by Barth as an affirmation of oneself as one who has been affirmed by God. The call for self-actualization is read analogically to mean actualize yourself as covenant partner of God in Jesus Christ, become who you are as one who is already forgiven, justified, and judged by God. Even Scriptural passages that seem to reject self-affirmation on behalf of self-denial ("For whosoever will save his life shall lose it")are nonetheless interpreted by Barth to uphold the higher aim of authentic self-affirmation, *saving* one's life, through losing it in the death of the old, inauthentic self. "Self-affirmation is thus at the root an act of obedience" to the command of God the Creator.[39]

For a more detailed discussion of specific applications of the analogy of faith to psychotherapy, however, we can only refer back to the previous delineation of our five analogies in Chapter II. Fuller elaboration of this effort must await more adequate development by practicing clinicians who see the therapeutic context from the perspective of a covenant ontology.

3. A CRITIQUE OF NATURAL ANALOGIES

When Barth so firmly insists that "natural theology is not in any sense the partner of the theology of the Word of God," he defines *natural theology* as "the doctrine of a union of man with God existing outside God's revelation in Jesus Christ."[40] Note that when Barth criticizes natural theology, he is also blasting the central thrust of the American tradition of pastoral care and counseling (Boisen, Dicks, Bonnell, Hiltner, Johnson, Wise, Tillich), which for two generations has been enamored with psychotherapy but with little consciousness of the need for sharper kerygmatic self-identity in Protestant theology. Such a softheaded latitudinarianism has shown "a basic readiness in almost every connexion to discover new analogies in the world."[41] We are determined that our dialogue with therapy not fall into such an uncritical rut, but that it hold to the strict procedure of *analogia fidei,* however tempting it may be to elaborate natural analogies of various sorts.

How easy it would be to misunderstand the whole in-

tention of our inquiry, if Barth's critique of natural theology were not carefully understood and assimilated. If our
project is viewed merely as a series of natural analogies
which read Godward from human processes, then we
might as well not waste the effort, since this has already
been done *ad nauseum* and hardly needs repetition. However, if our analogies are understood as proceeding from
the strict assumption that God is known only in his self-
disclosure and that we have no " point of contact " other
than that given by God himself, they will then be seen in
proper perspective as a challenge to all attempts to *combine* " the knowability of God in Jesus Christ with His
knowability in nature, reason and history," which Barth
rightly characterizes as a "trojan horse . . . already
drawn into the city." [42]

" All kinds of things might become analogous of God if
it were left to our wisdom or will . . . to claim this thing
or that as an analogy of God, discovering and proclaiming
one analogy here to-day and another there to-morrow." [43]
Barth is describing well the present predicament of theology vis-à-vis therapy. Without a clear kerygmatic self-
identity, we have simply looked around here and there and
somewhat uncritically suggested that this or that looks
similar, without anchorage in a consistent doctrine of
analogy.

Against the usual assumption of natural theology that
one can reason about God analogically only from the
known to the unknown, the God of the Biblical witness
constantly appears as One who shatters our prior expectations. Rather than reading the analogy Godward by saying
that first we have knowledge of interpersonal or impersonal processes and thereby we can know something of
God without his self-disclosure, the kerygma announces
that God himself has met us over against and in spite of all

our preconditions and anticipations.[44] He has reversed our expectations in the suffering Messiah who was scandalously born in a manger and died on a cross! Biblical reasoning about God seldom moves from the known to the unknown, but rather from the self-disclosure of the unexpected, unknown God to our knowing ourselves as having been known by him. He intrudes upon and negates all our previous inauthentic ways of supposedly "knowing" him and calls us to a radically new form of knowing, which judges and transforms all our former alleged self-knowledge. In the Biblical faith, we cannot reason from human knowns to the divine unknown. Rather, faith has learned to reason from the unknown to the known, from the holy God who has made himself known to a deeper perception of our already partially known historical and interpersonal relationships.

"How do we come to think, by means of our thinking, that which we cannot think at all by this means?" Barth asks. "How do we come to say, by means of language, that which we cannot say at all by this means?"[45] Of course we will use various words, ideas, constructs, borrowed from culture, but the basic point of the *analogia fidei* is not that our language reaches out for God, to lay hold of him in a more or less adequate way, but rather that the Kingdom of Heaven has come *to* us, and it is only out of this reality that we can respond in certain ways with our own always inadequate language. The comic example by which Barth likes best to show the freedom of God to choose his own means of self-presentation is the story of Balaam, where the Lord speaks through Balaam's *ass*, " as if incidentally to show that the divine possibility involved does not have either a limit, let alone a condition, in humanity."[46]

Despite strictures against natural theology, Barth frequently speaks of the universal scope of grace in creation: "Not only God's servants (Ps. 111:1), not only His saints (Ps. 145:10), not only Zion (Ps. 147:12), not only the house of Israel (Ps. 135:19), shall and may praise the Lord, but also the nations (Ps. 66:8; 117:1), all flesh (Ps. 145:21), everything that hath breath (Ps. 150:6), heaven and earth and sea (Ps. 69:34), sun and moon (Ps. 148:3), the angels of God (Ps. 103:20), all His works (Ps. 103:22)." [47] The essential core of Barth's doctrine of creation is that creation is the external basis of the covenant and the covenant is the internal basis of creation.[48] But however much divine revelation may be present in all creation, it is not perceived as such without knowing Jesus Christ as revealer of the covenant.[49]

We now proceed in our discussion of analogy with a critical examination of two alternative traditions of analogical reflection, the *analogia entis* of Thomist philosophy and the organismic analogies of process philosophy, both of which allege the knowability of God on the basis of natural analogies, which read Godward from human existence. The dialogue with therapy in the past decades owes much to these two analogical traditions, although their contribution has never been fully acknowledged by those who have put them to greatest use. We will clarify both styles of analogical thinking, relate them to the *analogia fidei* and to our thesis on psychotherapy.

4. THE CATHOLIC TRADITION OF ANALOGIA ENTIS

Although Barth's dialogue with Rome has always been in flux, "a bird in flight," it is evident that he is engaged in especially intense dialogue with the Thomist *analogia entis* as he develops his own doctrine of analogy. Barth reads the analogy of being in this way: "As himself a being, man is able to know a being as such. But if this is so,

then in principle he is able to know all being, even God as
the incomparably real being. Therefore . . . we must affirm his knowability apart from His revelation." [50] Thus the
traditional Thomist view of analogy is a principal example
of a natural theology at work on the problem of analogy,
consequently a prime target for Barthian polemic.

The Thomist analogy reads Godward from the concept
of being. " The basic proposition in the doctrine of Thom-
istic analogy, in its strict and proper meaning, is that whatever perfection is analogically common to two or more beings is intrinsically (formally) possessed by each, not,
however, by any two in the same way or mode, but by
each in proportion to its being." [51] Since God participates
in being perfectly, he is knowable analogically from the
knowledge of any being in which he participates. The
analogy rests on the proportion of the being in which one
participates. Since man can know something of finite being, he can know God as one who incomparably partici-
ates in finite being.

Barth's conflict with the *analogia entis* centers in his
crucial argument that God is known only in his self-disclosure, and therefore only in faith, and that knowledge of
God is not derivable from a general concept of being or
particular beings. His caveat is not wholly foreign to the
Catholic tradition itself, however, inasmuch as Thomas
Aquinas acknowledges, along with Augustine, that at best
man's knowledge of God is to know that he does not know
God adequately with his finite categories.[52] Thomas' own
theological *summa* culminates with a *pia confessio ignorantia* that God is above everything that one can say and
think about him, and that indeed God is best known by
us on earth as being unknown. According to one recent
Thomist interpreter, the *analogia entis,* when properly followed, does not intend to render knowledge of God, but

only knowledge of our human propositions. "What is proved is not the divine act of existing but the truth of our human proposition affirming that God or the purely actual exists." [53]

The ordinary pattern of reflection in the *analogia entis* is by comparison between things already understood and things not yet fully known. "In the comparative process, some relation of proportion must be discovered between the known and unknown if the frontier of knowledge is to be advanced." [54] But there is also another vital tradition of Catholic thinking which argues that because of God's infinite perfection, there can be no comparison between God and finite processes. If God is truly infinite and perfect, our ordinary ways of knowing simply do not provide the means for knowing him. Nicholas of Cusa thus proposed that the primary datum is our own *unknowing* or lack of knowledge of God and that any positive solution must respect and build out from this human situation. [55] Consequently the only way to think about God is a *via negativa*, reflecting by negation upon the radical limitations of human processes. This is remarkably similar to Bultmann's argument that man's natural knowledge of God is only negative knowledge of his lack of God, [56] which itself is consistent with Barth's critique of natural theology. Here Catholic and Protestant thinking meet.

Although we will not tediously repeat Barth's elaborate criticism of the *analogia entis* (cf. *CD*, II/1), it is at least necessary to note that forceful arguments have been set forth by distinguished Roman Catholic theologians to show that the *analogia fidei* is consistent with historic Catholic epistemology. If the thesis proposed by such Roman Catholic theologians as Gottlieb Söhngen proves defensible, the whole notion of *analogia entis* can be fittingly incorporated into the framework of *analogia fidei* without

contradiction of either. For Söhngen has welcomed the
analogy of faith as a legitimate statement of Catholic doctrine on the basis of the principle of *esse sequitur operari,*
that knowledge of being follows from knowledge of activity. If knowledge of the being of God must be subordi-
nated to the knowledge of God's activity, any use of *analogia entis* must be subordinate to an *analogia fidei,* since
one cannot reason about God's being except in relation to
God's action, which is only knowable in response to his
self-disclosure. If so, one cannot employ the *analogia entis*
apart from faith.[57]

We can learn much, as did Barth himself, from Anselm,
who sought to persuade both Jew and heathen of his theological proofs, but through a reasoning of faith which
never leaves behind its liberating presupposition. Likewise, if therapeutic empathy is in some way illuminated
by the self-disclosure of God, the task of theology is to
make it reasonable, or to make clear through human reasoning its divine reasonableness. Thus our entire exercise
intends to be a *fides quaerens intellectum,* a faith which
seeks to make itself intelligible.[58]

Although this brief review of the Catholic doctrine of
analogy lacks much detail, it may nevertheless serve to
show that the tension between Barth and the Catholic tradition in the earlier period of the *Dogmatics* may be
slightly ameliorated by a broader view of various Catholic doctrines of analogy and by an increasing willingness
of influential Catholic interpreters such as Balthasar,
Rahner, and Küng to view Barth's contribution as consistent with the deeper intention of Catholic theology.
Now we turn to another pattern of analogical reflection
which might be supposed as inimical to our effort, but
which upon examination may offer unexpected support for
our proposal, viz., process philosophy.

5. PROCESS ANALOGIES

Although Charles Hartshorne is usually thought to be on the opposite end of the theological spectrum from Karl Barth, he develops much of the same type of analogical thinking as that which we have found in Barth, viz., a form of analogy that sees all finite realities in their imperfection from the vantage point of the perfection of God who is absolutely relative, absolutely *related* to finite processes, sharing radically in temporal existence.

Note carefully the reasoning by which Hartshorne confirms Barth's analogy in this remarkable passage: " Concerning the question of literalness in theological concepts, I wish (with apologies to him) to urge Barth's procedure (when taken to task for treating God in terms of personality). He said, I believe, something like this: We know what personality is because we know God; our understanding of human ' personality ' is derived from revelation." [59] Hartshorne is here questioning Tillich's view that theology can speak of God only in symbolic terms. He replies that only God can be spoken of in literal terms and that all finite references must be symbolic. However different Barth and Hartshorne may be on the function of symbolic language in theology, they agree formally on the essential direction of analogical thinking.

Following Hartshorne's epistemology, one can best know what human empathy means even amid its broken forms, by reasoning analogically from the perfect empathy of God with the world. Unfortunately, however, Hartshorne has shown little interest in affirming the kerygmatic presupposition that this empathetic, reconciling love of God is adequately clarified only in a once for all event of the special historical self-disclosure of God incarnate, an event which judges and defines all other events of alleged revelation.

Theological analogies typically fail in one of three ways: "through vagueness, through inappropriateness, and through self-contradiction." Often a "vacillation arises, by which one avoids a too vague analogy only by falling into an objectionably anthropomorphic one, and then, when the anthropomorphism is noted, takes refuge again in the vagueness." [60] Predictably Hartshorne blames this quandary on an inadequate doctrine of God as totally immutable and proposes that "scholars are beginning to recognize that there is a way of avoiding this result, namely to admit that in some analogous if not univocal sense God is temporal and spatial." [61]

Hartshorne proposes three basic analogies, which, taken together, are appropriate for theology: "The *social* analogy (prominent in the idea of the divine fatherhood), that God is to us as a superior and benevolent human being is to other human beings; the *mind-body* analogy, that God is the soul of the universe as a man is the soul of so much of nature as is included within his skin; and the *artist* analogy, that God creatively produces and shapes the universe." [62] Although each analogy has its limitations, Hartshorne argues that "the most perfect possible analogy must somehow combine the merits and avoid the defects of these analogies. This can be done by supposing a relationship as intimate and *constant* as that between mind and body, as *sympathetic* as that between the ideal father and his child, and as *active* as that between artist and his materials." [63]

The remainder of our discussion of process theology will consist of an elaboration of these three analogies from the viewpoint of the *analogia fidei* as they apply to psychotherapy. Summarizing our proposition: As the relation of the redeeming God to the estranged world is constant, sympathetic, and active, and knowable as such in Jesus Christ, so is the relation of the congruent therapist to the troubled client constant, sympathetic, and active.

Hartshorne's three analogies, which we are roughly following in developing this schema, may be more broadly construed in the following manner:

HARTSHORNE'S ANALOGIES	MORE BROADLY CONSTRUED	THE INCLUSIVE CATEGORIES
The Social Analogy	I–Thou Relationships	*Inter*personal Processes
The Mind-Body Analogy	I–I Relationships	*Intra*personal Processes
The Artist Analogy	I–It Relationships	*Im*personal Processes

Instead of following Hartshorne's more restricted terminology, we will broaden the focus to develop allegedly inclusive categories. Taken together and properly understood, we hypothesize that these three analogies are comprehensive constructs and may provide a comprehensive theory of theological analogy, since there can be no conceivable relationship in which a person exists which cannot be subsumed under one or more of the categories of interpersonal, intrapersonal, and impersonal processes.

a. The *interpersonal* analogy, or social analogy, likens the relation between God and the world to that of two persons in a caring, giving, and receiving interaction, as typified by the relation of father and son.[64] Although the loving father and the beloved son aptly communicate this correspondence, we would suggest that *any* authentic interpersonal relationship, whether brother and brother, friend and friend, lover and beloved, etc., actually may become useful or meaningful as an analogy of faith in response to God's self-disclosure. We need not unnecessarily confine ourselves to the special relation of father and son, since any authentic I–Thou relationship can reflect the love, care, and understanding of God. The analogy of faith, however, typically reads the correspondence manward from God's self-disclosure rather than merely as a natural analogy: God has met us in ways which, when we look for ordinary human language to speak of his love, care, help, and friendship toward us, quite spontaneously turn us toward concrete interpersonal relationships of loving, caring, healing, and friendship in order to express the reality by which we understand ourselves ultimately to have been grasped. God is thus spoken of as true Father, divine deliverance as an act of brotherly compassion, redemption as a deed of divine friendship. "What language shall I borrow," writes Paul Gerhardt, "to thank Thee, dearest Friend?" Interpersonal analogies abound in the Biblical response to God's self-disclosure.

Consequently, when therapists describe unconditional positive regard, acceptance, prizing the neighbor, etc., it is only quite typical for the community of faith to seize upon such processes as expressions of authentic healing, redeeming, interpersonal relationships, which in some sense reflect the healing, delivering, redemptive activity of God. It is not that God's activity is somehow clarified by psychotherapy, but that psychotherapy seems to express something which faith has already deeply experienced in its relation to the salvation event to which it witnesses as its ground and source. Consequently, faith reasons analogically that we can best know the depth dimension of unconditional positive regard by looking at the event and person in which this healing reality is prototypically and ultimately manifested in human history. We know what authentic fatherhood is by knowing our own sonship in Jesus Christ. We know most profoundly what an authentic therapeutic relationship involves because we have been met by an authentic divine therapeutic relationship in the Christ event. To summarize: The character of all authentic interpersonal relationships, including psychotherapy, is illumined by the style of God's own caring, affirming, unconditional acceptance and positive regard for our estranged human condition in Jesus Christ.

b. The *intrapersonal* analogy argues that God is to the world as the mind is to the body. We wish to substitute for Hartshorne's terms mind and body, two Rogerian constructs: *self* and *organism.*[65] If we accept this substitution, which we believe to be appropriate to Hartshorne's intention, we can now read the analogy as follows: *God is to the world as the self is to its organismic experiencing process.*

In therapy, of course, the basic construct that describes the relation of self and organismic experiencing is *congruence,* wherein the self with its self-image, self-identity, self-understanding congrues or harmonizes with, and is in touch with, its feeling process, its organismic experiencing. We refer here to the previous discussion in which we have already spelled out the analogy between the divine congruence and therapeutic congruence, arguing that historic Christian theology has attempted to speak in trinitarian language of the divine congruence, or the self-identity of God in the midst of his participation in the estrangement of the world. The trinitarian thought that God is not fragmented amid his functioning as creator, redeemer, and consummator, that God continues to be himself as he shares in human estrangement, is a basically illuminating analogy for the congruence of the therapist or any man who participates in estrangement without himself being estranged.

Hartshorne understandably places high priority on the intrapersonal (mind-body) analogy as the most defensible one by which theology can understand the intimate re-

lation of God and the world, always, however, with the
acknowledgment that it needs the correction and completion of the interpersonal analogy to amend its nonsocial,
undialogical implications.[66] The fatal limitation of the social analogy is that friend and friend or father and son
can be conceived as existing quite separately, whereas
faith cannot finally imagine God and the world as separate. This is corrected by the image of the intimate relation of God to the world as expressed in the self and
organism analogy.

Again, however, it is necessary to make clear that we
are not reading this as a natural analogy. We must press
the question: Is God knowable simply from the human
mind-body analogy, or is the human self and organism
finally understandable following the *analogia fidei* only
from God's relation to the world? Is the analogy to be
read Godward from intrapersonal processes, or is it to
be read manward from the divine being? For Hartshorne
it can be read either way, although the direction from
God to the world is logically and epistemologically prior.
We are electing, along with Barth, to read the analogy
only in the manward direction, exclusively from the self-
disclosure of God to intrapersonal and interpersonal
processes. It should be underscored, however that Hartshorne's concept of literal knowledge of God and symbolic knowledge of the world tends, curiously enough, to
move much more in the direction of *analogia fidei* than
analogia entis. Although due to their differing views of
revelation, Barth and Hartshorne are poles apart in the
way they give content to the analogy, *formally* their
analogical procedure is remarkably similar.

c. The *impersonal* analogy, which argues that God is to
the world as an artisan shaping inorganic materials, is the
most difficult to apply to psychotherapy, since therapy is

much more an intra- and interpersonal relationship than
impersonal. Effective therapy strongly resists the attitude that the person is merely an object, a case to be investigated, tested, diagnosed, and analyzed, a machine to
be repaired. We readily agree with Hartshorne that this
analogy is less useful for understanding the action of God
and for understanding psychotherapy, despite its pre-
dominance in the history of theology with its flood of
familiar images portraying God as worker, repairman,
renovator, shaper, and controller of natural objects or
processes. The basic limitation of the artisan analogy is
that it perpetuates the defects of both the inter- and
intrapersonal analogies without adding significantly to
them.[67] It views the objective material as separable from
the artisan, and it lacks the full dimension of interpersonal dialogue which is characteristic of the Biblical understanding of God and man. It does, however, dramatize
the active intiative of God in shaping worldly processes.

If correlated with the other two analogies, the artisan
analogy may be developed to apply in some fashion to the
psychotherapeutic process under the analogy of faith as
follows: As the artist shapes raw materials into some
meaningful or beautiful image, as the artisan creates or
repairs the watch, the dam or the computer, likewise the
client in therapy is involved in the process of creating,
reshaping, and renovating himself as a human being. This
process is most profoundly viewed, however, under the
broader prospect of God's own intention to create, re-
shape, and renovate human existence, as witnessed to in
the kerygma. As God is constantly active in the process
of redemption of the created order, so is the therapeutic
process understandable as an expression of human re-
formation, restoration, re-creation. Rodin's statue of man
creating himself, with mallet in hand, chiseling himself

into being, expresses the essence of psychotherapy! Again, however, we must insist that the analogy be read man-ward from revelation instead of Godward from natural processes. We are proposing not that we learn of God's new creation simply from observing the natural process of human creativity, but rather that God has revealed himself as Re-creator so as to enable faith to reconceive the meaning of the very human processes in which something broken is being fixed, something new and original is being shaped out of chaotic, unformed materials.

We have now defined and limited the *analogia fidei,* illustrating it and applying it to the process of psychotherapy with certain ominous warnings about its propensity for misuse, relating it to two other analogical procedures derived from the Thomist and process philosophical traditions. These two traditions have been heavily relied upon, however unconsciously, to develop the last generation of dialogue between psychotherapy and theology, and to bring it to its present predicament and promise. We can only wish that perceptive process theologians would provide something of the same sort of creative Christological redirection which has already been provided for the *analogia entis* by Söhngen, Balthasar, Küng, and others.[68] Far from being inimical to the *analogia fidei,* both Thomist and process analogies can be illuminated and elaborated through a fresh dialogue with a theology of revelation and faith's analogy.

6. A Stern Word on Worldly Dialogue

In his perceptive treatment of "The Knowability of God," Barth devotes a long section of his dogmatics [69] to a discussion of the appropriate basis of dialogue with the world. Often the church is advised to begin its conversation with the world by looking for some *point of contact*

where something is already familiar to the mind of natural
man. If only this foothold can be obtained, he can be
addressed by grace. Thus it is purported to be the duty
of Christian apologetics to take this initial step toward
the natural man with the following strategy in mind: " In
a sense, it will have to play with him in order to convince
him in a wise and friendly manner of the fact that after
all it is *only a game*, and in order to prepare him for that
which it does take seriously, and to which it wants to
lead him." [70]

Should this be our stance with the therapist? Are we to
play a game with him, concealing our central kerygmatic
presupposition of the event of love of God in Christ, in
order that we can lead him beyond a preliminary stage
and finally place before him some actual proclamation
concerning God's verdict and claim upon his present situation? If so, natural theology must be a necessary prelude
to any theology or proclamation.

Barth answers that we must not think we have won a
victory if we engage the discussion on the basis of some
common point of contact which in itself displays a basic
misunderstanding of the actual situation of man. Such
are pyrrhic victories. Honest Christian dialogue with the
world can never wear a phony smile just to get a foot in
the door. [71]

When we approach secular therapy with a credulous
affirmation that we are " taking man seriously by con-
firming his independence," this may not be serious at all,
but an empty masquerade. Christian faith does not begin
to take the man whom God has loved seriously merely by
viewing him strictly from within the limited view of his
own self-determination and insight! Instead it seeks to
refocus the issue in all strictness upon the confession that
there is no actual man with whom we can deal at all apart

from his participation in Jesus Christ, nor any "man as such" who can be known apart from God and his self-disclosure. "There is only the man for whom Jesus Christ has died and risen again, whose affairs He has taken into his own hands. And everything that it has to say to man can only be an explanation of this his true existence." [72]

If this is so, then a great deal of our supposed conversation with therapy has not been true dialogue at all, but mere monologue in which theology has mutely listened to the therapist's views and echoed them without ever clearly disclosing the distinctive beginning point from which all Christian worship and thought proceeds, viz., the self-disclosure of God in creation and redemption as the basis for understanding the human condition and possibility. Until we begin to be honest with the therapist and clarify for him the point at which we begin to reflect seriously upon the human situation, our dialogue is going to be little more than self-deceit and illusion, which falls short of the congruence of which the therapist so ably speaks.

The sophisticated secular man, such as the psychotherapist, is "not a child playing games, to whom we are in the habit of speaking down in order the more surely to raise him up." We must not pretend that therapists are so dull or unperceptive as not to see some incongruity in such a deceitful witness. "Unbelief . . . is far too strongly and far too inwardly orientated to the truth, and (even if only negatively) interested in it, for us to be able to convince it of its wrongness and confront it with the truth by a skilful handling of what is after all, however preliminary and pedagogic in intention, further untruth." [73]

If the psychotherapeutic tradition has often sported a frankly agnostic or atheistic garb, theology might be well advised to follow the same remarkable counsel that Barth offers to East German Christians when confronted by less subtle forms of atheism in their Communist regime: "You should accept none of your countrymen at their own estimate. Don't ever honor them as the unbelieving and strong men they pretend to be! . . . They are just posing as the strong men they would like to be! Rather, you must meet their unbelief with a joyous unbelief in their attempted atheism. You as Christians must confidently claim that your atheists belong to God as much as you do. Whether they will be converted . . . is a secondary question. What is certain is that God is not against them, but for them." [74]

Barth shows the fatal consequence of wearing a mask in this conversation: "Now, suppose the partner in the conversation discovers that faith is trying to use the well-known artifice of dialectic in relation to him. We are not taking him seriously because we withhold from him what we really want to say and represent. It is only in appearance that we devote ourselves to him, and therefore what we say to him is only an apparent and unreal statement. What will happen then? Well, not without justice — although misconstruing the friendly intention which perhaps motivates us — he will see himself despised and deceived, and indeed doubly despised and deceived. He will shut himself up and harden himself against the faith which does not speak out frankly, which deserts its own standpoint and merely pretends to take up the contrary standpoint of unbelief. What use to unbelief is a faith which obviously knows different?" [75] Let us suppose, on the other hand, that the partner in dialogue does not know that the Christian witness is wearing a mask! Suppose there occur decisions, conversations, and teachings corresponding to this faith which is masked as unbelief! Suppose the person responds to what he believes is the church's true proclamation, only later to find it an empty deceit. Such disasters can be avoided only by obeying the commandment: " Thou shalt not bear false witness."

The Christian kerygma is free to utilize secular language to announce the good news: " It is definitely not the case that confession must always be made in biblical words or in the language of Zion. But it is also not the case that this is to be anxiously and deliberately avoided ('How shall I put it to my children?'). In free defiance, it often may and must choose the language of Zion. But it will not be bound to it. It often may and must choose wholly secular language." [76] Above all, amid this dialogue, the Christian community is called to be " human and natural in its very Christianity. . . . Thus its strictly Christian character can flourish only on the soil of a serious and *cheerful secularity*, yet, on the other hand, it can live a meaningful human and worldly life only as this has an unassuming but self-evident Christian impress." [77] Although we must leave it to a subsequent discussion to elaborate a new style of worldly dialogue with psychotherapy, its essential lines are already well staked out by these perceptive comments of the preeminent theologian of our times.

CHAPTER V

KERYGMA AND THERAPEIA

Our thesis has been that effective secular psychotherapy implicitly assumes an accepting reality which is made explicit in the Christian kerygma. We now conclude our study with a brief exegetical analysis of key Biblical terms relating to our thesis, examining what the Biblical witness has to say about the healing realities at work in the world in relation to the coming reign of God.

One essential aim of this final chapter is to show that *psychotherapy is not a modern concept* at all, however up-to-date it may sound, but rather a pervasive concern of the Biblical witness and indeed of the whole ancient world, if we mean by psychotherapy its historic connotation, of service rendered to man in his internal self-relation, *therapeia* for the *psyche,* the attentive careful helping of the self toward authentic internal existence. Although this term has been temporarily captured by the interests of modern medical professionalism, and though its current meanings in English chiefly have a medical reference, its broader root meanings in ancient Greek and in the Biblical witness freight deep significance for a renewed and more profound understanding of the healing process.

Therefore we intend to focus upon the fascinating ety-

mology of the term *therapeia*, especially as it relates to
the New Testament proclamation of the reign of God,
showing how the kerygma announces a final end-time
therapeutic (!) event of God's caring service to humanity,
to nurture man toward health and authenticity. We will
also clarify certain key Biblical terms that have cognates
in current psychotherapy, such as *paraklēsis*, in order to
illuminate the exegetical substructure underneath our argument. It is not merely as an afterthought that we un-
dertake this difficult exegetical effort, but indeed as a
climactic consummation of the entire argument already
set forth, which we hope has proceeded throughout on
sound exegetical grounds, but which we now intend to
make fully transparent.

1. THERAPEIA AS ATTENTIVE, CARING SERVICE

The root word for " therapy," the Greek *therapeia*, with
its derivatives *therapōn, therapeuō,* and *therapontos,* has
an intriguing etymological history which bears some illuminating meanings for current psychotherapy. *Therapeia* means " service." [1] The noun appears commonly in
the writings of Aristotle, Hippocrates, Philo, and Josephus.
More particularly, it means attentive, caring service, the
kind of heedful, scrupulous, conscientious care that one
would hope to receive in private and intimate matters,
such as medical service. The *therapōn* is the servant who
renders careful, experienced, watchful, meticulous, skilled,
obedient, painstaking service to the one to whom he is
intimately responsible. *Therapeia* is used in such widely
varied contexts as the service of one who cares for dead
bodies, one who skillfully tailors clothing, or even a bar-
ber who renders his meticulous service to his client. *Therapeia* is thus much broader than merely medical care. Anyone who serves, waits upon, helps, and attends to the

personal needs of another is a *therapōn*.[2]

It is significant that the closest Greek synonym for *therapōn* is *diakonos*, also meaning " servant," from which has come our term " deacon " and the whole concept of the diaconate ministry. Thus it is evident from the outset that there is a close linguistic similarity between the concepts of therapist and minister. In fact in the ancient world, *therapeia* was frequently translated into Latin as *ministerium*. Of the several Greek words signifying " servant " (*therapōn, diakonos, oiketēs, pais,* and *doulos*), the most intimate of these is *therapōn,* which always refers to some highly personal, sympathetic, confidential act of service, in contrast to *doulos,* which bespeaks more the distance between servant and master.[3]

It is not surprising, therefore, that medical service, a very intimate form of personal care, should be considered also as *therapeia.* We wish to emphasize, however, this crucial etymological finding which we believe to be profoundly suggestive for current psychotherapy: that authentic *therapeia* in its original meaning, whether rendered by the physician, mortician, household servant, tailor, or valet, means attentive, caring, intimate skilled *service.*

If linguistic roots are in any sense meaningful or illuminating for present-day functioning, then we are led to observe that any authentic therapy is going to be essentially a serving relationship in which the therapist is at the disposal of the client to provide attentive, skilled, meticulous care for his special needs. He who has special skills in listening, in being deeply attentive to the feelings of others, who can patiently wait upon others without frustration or hostility, will probably be the most effective *therapōn.* It is not surprising, therefore, that one of the most consistent marks of the effective modern psychotherapist is that of being an attentive listener, able to focus his total concentration upon the internal frame of reference of the person to whom he is responsible.

In an age when psychotherapy, like all medical service, is so frequently associated with a sterile, impersonal, expert, technical, mechanistic, and often mercenary professional image, it is somewhat surprising that the root word for therapy should be the simple image of the servant. This seems an appropriate place, however, to begin to rethink the basic process of psychotherapy and is fully consonant with the views of the best therapists.

If the word " psychotherapy " rings in our ears as a fresh contemporary sound like " automation," " penicillin," or " cybernetics," it needs to be shown forthrightly that it is not a new concept at all, but an ancient concern of human history. It simply combines two very common words in the ancient world, which were frequently used in close interrelation: *psychē* and *therapeia*, a special caring service rendered at the level of the inner depths of man's existence, the *psychē*. Although usually translated " soul," *psychē* has recently received more explicit existential reinterpretation as " that human state of being alive which inheres in man as a striving, willing, purposing self." [4] *Psychē* may be variously translated " vitality," or simply " life " itself, just as it may take on the fuller meaning of " person " or " self." But whether rendered soul, life principle, the feelings and emotions, or the " seat and center of the inner life of man in its many varied aspects," [5] in any case *psychē* points essentially to the depths of personal internal human existence, a dimension where *therapeia* of the most skilled and intimate sort is often profoundly needed. Thus the concern to render a meaningful *therapeia* to a man's *psychē*, a service to human self-understanding at the center of vitality of the human organism, is a persistent and urgent theme of the New Testament and much ancient literature.

In the New Testament the prototypical image of the *therapōn* is Jesus Christ, the person and event of God's own intimate, healing, restoring service to human history (Matt. 9:1-8; Mark 1:32-34; Luke 4:18). God himself is *therapōn*, according to the kerygma. The *therapeia* which he renders is the mediation of divine redemptive love, dramatized in the exorcism of demonic powers, and once for all clarified in the events of the last days of Jesus' ministry. Repeatedly Jesus is recognized as a *therapōn* who serves and cares for the broken and sick (Matt. 8:7; 4:24; Mark 1:34; 3:10; Luke 14:3).[6] When the crippling demonic spirits recognized the power of his *therapeia*, they were among the first to learn the secret of his Messianic identity, and to cry out: " You are the Son of God! " (Mark 3:11; Luke 4:41.)

The question of whether it is lawful to render *therapeia* on the Sabbath became a burning issue in the ministry of Jesus (Matt. 12:1-14; Mark 3:1-6; Luke 6:1-11), curiously parallel to the current issue of the relation of psychotherapy to traditional religious structures. The predominate religious tradition at the time of Jesus' ministry did not want to see any *therapeia* on the Sabbath Day. They wanted it to be an entirely secular function.[7] *Therapeia* was thought to have nothing to do with the promised salvation of Israel. When Jesus answered that the Sabbath was made for man, not man for the Sabbath, and that it is lawful to do good on the Sabbath (Matt. 12:8; 12:12; Mark 2:27; Luke 6:6-11), and when he offered *therapeia* on the Sabbath as a sign of the emerging reign of God, thus intruding upon the holy day with his ministry to sick bodies and souls and erasing the strict boundary between sacred and secular functions, this caused the greatest offense among the religious professionals, who "immediately held counsel with the Herodians against him, how to destroy him" (Mark 3:6). The touchy issue of whether *therapeia* is properly a sign of the coming reign of God points us directly toward our next question, which focuses upon the precise relation of *kerygma* and *therapeia*.

2. KERYGMA AND THE HEALING EVENT

"Kerygma" means "proclamation."[8] Distinguished from teaching (*didaskein, didachē*), which is concerned more with the communication of *ideas,* the verb *kēryssein* has to do with the announcement of an *event,* which in the New Testament centers in the event of God's occurring love.[9] The Christian kerygma thus points toward an occurrence, the Christ event, by which faith understands itself to have been grasped by the *therapeia* of God himself. Kerygma witnesses to the saving presence of the divine *therapōn* amid human history, the reign of God's own healing ministry to man.

A *kēryx* (proclaimer) is quite different from a *therapōn* in that he is responsible for bringing to public attention urgent announcements of events that bear illuminating significance for human life. His task is more overt and public than the more intimate, personal, meticulous task of the *therapōn*. "A *kēryx* may be a town crier, an auctioneer, a herald, or anyone who lifts up his voice and claims public attention to some definite thing he has to announce."[10] The *kēryx* has more in common with modern vocations connected with mass media communications or with the postal service (bringers of news) than with the roles of either the modern parish minister or the psychotherapist. The early church borrowed the term "kerygma" and its cognates from ordinary koine Greek and applied it to a specific event, the announcement of the coming of

God into the world as savior, the good news that Jesus is the Christ, the expected deliverer. The *kēryx* announced, not the *idea* of healing, but the *event* of the healing of human history, the self-disclosure of the One who enables all secular healing.

Kerygma complements *therapeia* by witnessing overtly to the hidden source of healing, the God of all comfort. Whereas *therapeia* wordlessly witnesses to the reign of God through the *events* of the exorcism of demonic powers, *kerygma* involves the explicit clarification of the meaning of these events (Matt. 9:18-35). *Therapeia* without *kerygma* would be like an unannounced wedding feast, the election of a President which never made the newspapers, a world record established but never reported by television, a great plague conquered but the name of the wonder drug never announced.

Mark well that the verb *kēryssein* meant to announce something to persons who had not already heard it! [11] It would do little good for a *kēryx* repeatedly to publish news of the ending of a war to folk who already knew it was over. Thus *kerygma* involved an exciting, urgent mission of announcement of good news, not just to the church but to *the world* — the Gentiles! By analogy, the modern *kēryx* is commissioned not only to retell the good news to people who have already heard it (the church), but is more so urgently sent out to announce the good news of God's healing presence to the secularized man of our time (who, it can be argued, is epitomized by the psychotherapist)! Genuine evangelization does not mean, as it has tended to be reduced by Protestant pietism, merely the delivering of sermons to the converted community, but more so the announcement of the good news of God's healing action to the outsider, the estranged, the secularized, worldly man to whom it is equally addressed. If evangelism is often narrowly regarded as getting people *out* of the world and into the pious community, its original meaning involved much more a serious dialogue with the world with the aim of communicating good news at the very point at which the world does its work (Matt. 9:35; 28:19). In the case of psychotherapy this means the actual process of the therapeutic help.

The Servant-Messiah was remembered as one who uniquely blended the dual ministries of *kerygma* and *therapeia* in genuine involvement with the world. He "went throughout all Galilee, preaching in their synagogues and casting out demons." (Mark 1:39.) Great multitudes of people came "to *hear* him and to be *healed* of their diseases" (Luke 6:17). "Now when the sun was setting, all those who had any that were sick with various diseases brought them to him; and he laid his hands on every one of them and *healed* them. . . . He said to them, 'I must *preach* the good news of the kingdom of God to the other cities also; for I was sent for this purpose.'" (Luke 4:40-43.)

The twofold thrust of the apostolic mission is summarized in Jesus' instructions to the Twelve: "And preach [*kēryssete*] as you go, saying, 'The kingdom of heaven is at hand.' Heal [*therapeute*] the sick, raise the dead, cleanse lepers, cast out demons" (Matt. 10:7-8). According to Luke's Gospel, "They departed and went through the villages, preaching [*euangelizomenoi*] the gospel and healing [*therapeuontes*] everywhere" (Luke 9:6). In the sending of the seventy, their commission included the same dual focus: "Heal the sick . . . and say to them, 'The Kingdom of God has come near to you'" (Luke 10:8). It seems to be a very deliberate matter that *therapeia* and *kerygma* are conjoined in a single mission of service and witness. The chief clues to the Messianic presence were the proclamation of the now impending reign of God and the *therapeia* of the Servant-Messiah.

Matthew summarizes the mission of Jesus in the three-fold form of teaching, preaching, and healing: "And he went about all Galilee, teaching [*didaskōn*] in their synagogues and preaching the gospel [*euangelion*] of the kingdom and healing [*therapeuōn*] every disease and every infirmity among the people, . . . and they brought him all the sick, those afflicted with various diseases and pains, demoniacs, epileptics, and paralytics, and he healed them" (Matt. 4:23-24). Any *therapeia* rendered on behalf of the coming reign of God exists properly in the context of Christian *euangelion* and *didachē*. The threefold ministry of *didachē*, *euangelion*, and *therapeia* remains today as a concise summary of the mission of the church.

However much it may offend the finer sensibilities of staid churchmen, Jesus gave to the church explicit therapeutic authority (*exousia*) to "heal every disease and every infirmity" (*therapeuein pasan noson!*, Matt. 10:1). Luke's narrative reads: "He called the twelve together and gave them power and authority over all demons and to cure diseases [*therapeuein*], and he sent them out to preach [*kēryssein*] the kingdom of God and to heal" (Luke 9:1-2). Again it is not accidental that the two principal terms of our discussion are closely linked together: *therapeia* and *kerygma*. For *therapeia* is a mighty sign of the presence of God's reconciling power amid the world. When questioned on the meaning of his therapeutic ministry, Jesus declared, "If it is by the finger of God that I cast out demons, then the kingdom of God has come upon you" (Luke 11:20).

When John the Baptist heard of the *therapeia* of Jesus, he sent his disciples to ask: "Are you he who is to come, or shall we look for another?" Whatever might be the motivation of John's question, it is clear that Jesus answered it by pointing directly to his therapeutic activity as a sign of his Messianic vocation. He simply points to what he has been doing (*therapeia!*). His actions proclaim his mission (cf. Fuchs).[12] Without words, the therapeutic deeds proclaim his Messianic identity: "Go and tell John what you have seen and heard: the blind receive their sight, the lame walk, lepers are cleansed, and the deaf hear, the dead are raised up, the poor have good news preached to them. And blessed is he who takes no offense at me" (Luke 7:22-23). *Therapeia* thus validates *kerygma*. It is thus a mighty manifestation of the presence of the expected deliverer and an authentication of the reign of God. Likewise in psychotherapy today, it is everywhere evident that the anxious are being comforted, the depressed encouraged, the hostile reconciled, the psychotic welcomed to reality, and neurotic conflicts are being resolved! Whether it occurs in a religious or secular setting, such healing is still a sign of the eschatological presence of the reign of God's eternal accepting love.

3. THE COMFORT OF GOD

Several key Biblical passages will now help to illuminate the relationship between *kerygma* and *therapeia*, especially as they relate to current secular psychotherapy. We hope in these final pages to allow the Scripture to make clear its own witness on the issues we have been discussing.

Since the Biblical witness abounds in passages that impinge upon our thesis, we are compelled to be extremely selective in the ones that we examine in detail. We prefer, however, to choose a limited number of citations and give them more serious attention rather than string together a long thread of Scriptural references without proper exegesis. The two passages to which we wish to give the most serious attention are found in Paul's Corinthian correspondence. If the most dramatic account of Jesus as *therapōn* is found in the Lucan narrative, the most penetrating statement of God as the source of understanding and comfort is found in the Pauline letters. So we turn now to the two selections that best set forth the analogy of faith concerning God's comforting care, I Cor., ch. 13, and II Cor., ch. 1.

The noted passage on love in the thirteenth chapter of I Corinthians dramatically sharpens the procedure by which the analogy of faith views the process of empathetic understanding in this formula: *"Then I shall understand fully, even as I have been fully understood"* (I Cor. 13:12). If *now* means one's present situation of imperfect knowledge, and *then* refers to the hoped-for renewal of the self in the presence of unconditional love, it is only *then* that one shall understand fully, for love transcends knowledge. But one is then freed to understand himself and others because he has been understood. By whom? Hopefully by other finite human brothers, but by them only as representatives of the accepting empathetic love of God. Such love, or at least some vaguely mirrored manifestation of it, is the precondition of genuine understanding (I Cor. 13:2, 12). If you have all knowledge of pathological processes, even prophetic powers to analyze, diagnose, give Rorschach tests, and project future syndromes, and if you even understand all mysteries like transference and resistance, but do not have love, you gain nothing. Even if one is armed with all these scientific accouterments, testing devices, and diagnostic tools, etc., and adds to them faith, even a faith "to remove mountains," but has not love, it does not help.

Paul then clarifies the character and attitude of the

unconditional love (*agapē*) which preconditions understanding (*epiginōskō*). It is patient and kind, not jealous or boastful. It is not arrogant or rude. Above all, it does not insist upon its own way. It is patient with the compulsive defensiveness and resistance of the troubled neighbor. It is willing to be led in the direction in which the incongruent man intuits to be his deepest interest. It is not irritable or resentful. It rejoices not in wrong, but rejoices in the right, in personal growth and reconciliation. It is not accidental that Paul's description of *agapē* sounds curiously similar to the Rogerian account of unconditional positive regard, for the latter is unconsciously rooted in the former.

This is what love does: It bears all things, believes all things, hopes all things, endures all things. It projects itself phenomenologically into the sphere of reference of the neighbor's inner life and receives him, believes his word about himself, hopes all things for him which he most truly hopes for himself, yearns with him in his authentic intentions, shares with him all things, and endures with him through his quiet afflictions.

Such empathetic love shares in a reality which never ends, since it is grounded in being itself. Knowledge, psychometrics, esoteric language, all pass away, but not unconditional empathetic love. For it is rooted in reality itself. In our immaturity we reason from certain limited perspectives, but as we mature in faith and learn increasingly the meaning of empathetic positive regard, we find ourselves astonishingly rooted in the eternal reality of God's own love. Thus Paul writes: "When I was a child, I spoke like a child, I thought like a child, I reasoned like a child; when I became a man, I gave up childish ways" (I Cor. 13:11). Becoming a man means to live in the reality of God's acceptance and to reflect maturely the love and goodness of God. If now we see in a mirror dimly, *then* (in the presence of accepting love) we will see face to face. If now we live in the context of distorted, clouded interpersonal and intrapersonal relationships, then, insofar as we exist in the presence of a final unconditional empathetic love, we see face to face, we stand before one another, free to be ourselves and to look clearly at ourselves.

Paul concludes this passage with his incisive analogy of faith which reads: " Then I shall understand fully, even as I have been fully understood " (I Cor. 13:13). Self-understanding exists in the light of our being finally understood by God. To whatever degree we are able to understand our own humanity, faith knows that our humanity has always already been fully understood by God in Jesus Christ and that this is the ontological grounding of whatever penultimate understanding we might achieve of ourselves and of others.

The Greek word *paraklēsis* is usually translated " comfort " or " consolation," although its meanings actually range widely and move toward the connotation of empathetic understanding. Although the image of God as comforter, encourager, and consoler is a frequent one in Scripture, we will narrow our focus upon one particular text which best illuminates the relation of *kerygma* and *therapeia,* viz., the ascription at the beginning of Paul's second letter to Corinth.

The three parts of this salutation summarize the comforting activity of God as follows: (*a*) that God is the source of all comfort, (*b*) that we ourselves have been comforted by God, and (*c*) that we are called and enabled to share with others who are afflicted, the comfort with which we ourselves are comforted by God (II Cor. 1:3-4). That this is a very carefully constructed, precise theolog-

ical formulation is evident from its rhythmically balanced
clauses and frequent alliteration,[13] employing the word
paraklēsis and its derivatives ten times in five verses. The
central theme of this salutation is the *Deus totius consola-
tionis*, the God of all comfort, the Father of all mercies, the
source of never-ending compassion. Since this Scripture
resonates so well with everything else we have been trying to say, and in fact summarizes the whole thesis of this
book in a simple *locus classicus*, we will examine it phrase
by phrase as the prototypical example of the analogy of
faith applied to the therapeutic process.

The ascription is addressed to the Father of our Lord
Jesus Christ, the Father of mercies and God of all comfort.
Wherever we meet mercy in the broken world, there faith
celebrates its source and giver as the " God and Father
of our Lord Jesus Christ." Wherever comfort and consolation are present, their source is fully disclosed in the ministry of the merciful servant.

The second affirmation is that this same *Deus totius con-
solationis* has met us with comfort (*paraklēseōs*) in all our
affliction (v. 4). The base out of which we operate in offer-
ing *paraklēsis* to others is the existential awareness of our
own reception of the comfort of God. The word for affliction (*thlipsis*) means literally to be crushed, to be in a
narrow straight, a tight spot, between a rock and a hard
place. Its Latin equivalent, *pressura*, expresses a feeling
well known to psychotherapy, the experience of being
crushed by the weight of circumstances, " up against it,"
caught in a tight situation where the possibilities for self-
fulfillment are limited or nil.[14] Wherever such affliction is
experienced, one is allegedly being given the opportunity
to learn of the *paraklēsis* of God. Through the poetic device of alliteration, the text emphasizes the universality
and continuity of the comfort of God in *all* extremities.

God is the source of *all* comfort, our comforter in *all* afflictions, who enables us to comfort others in *any* affliction. There is no measure to his *paraklēsis*, since it is eternal and eschatologically given once for all in the Christ event.

The third part of the salutation draws the analogical conclusion prepared for in the first two affirmations. A superb illustration of the *analogia fidei*, it declares that if the God of all comfort has comforted us, *therefore*, we are called to *comfort others in affliction with the comfort with which we ourselves have been comforted by God*. (II Cor. 1:4; cf. Phil. 2:5-11; Col. 3:13; I John 4:10-11.) Just as we are to serve, forgive, and love as we have been served, forgiven, and loved by God himself in Jesus Christ, so are we to comfort. He who is grasped by the comfort of God is freed and called to comfort others. The therapeutic relationship we mediate is an expression of the *therapeia* by which God has so attentively cared for us. The positive regard we offer to the estranged neighbor is a response to the unconditional positive regard of God for us in our estrangement.

But what is the content of our sharing? Specifically *what* do we share — merely our own finite consolation, insight, and reassurance? Rather, we share the same sort of supportive, caring, understanding encouragement (*paraklēsis*) that God himself has shared with us. We " share with them the consolation we ourselves receive from God," as the New English Bible quite simply renders it. We comfort them " with the comfort with which we ourselves are comforted by God " (RSV). The best we can offer the disconsolate is the *paraklēsis* by which we have been divinely comforted, flowing through us in our personal interaction with the neighbor. " As Christ's cup of suffering overflows, and we suffer with him, so also through Christ our consolation overflows." (II Cor. 1:5, NEB.) It is the overflowing *therapeia* of God which our cup has received to over-flowing and which we pass on overflowing into the need of the neighbor. God's gracious sufficiency moves from himself to us, and through us to the neighbor. " Indeed, experience shows that the more we share Christ's suffering, the more we are able to give of his encouragement." (II Cor. 1:5, Phillips.) Our own personal afflictions thus take their place within the broader context of God's redeeming action, and suffering loses its power to subvert human health when seen within the framework of God's *paraklēsis*, so that for those who love the Lord, everything works for the good (Rom. 8:28).

Note, however, that neither the agent of comfort nor the afflicted are delivered from the affliction, but instead both are comforted *amid* the affliction. The promise of this ascription is not that faith is transported beyond the bounds of suffering, but that suffering itself can become a guide to authenticity, a means of grace.[15] Elsewhere Paul speaks of suffering as a context of rejoicing, not in a masochistic sense, but in the knowledge that " endurance produces character, and character produces hope, and hope does not disappoint us, because God's love has been poured into our hearts through the Holy Spirit which has been given to us " (Rom. 5:4-5).

Here in this single apostolic salutation, we thus find a concise précis of the whole shape of our argument, summarized in these three dimensions: God is known in Christ as the source of all comfort, who meets us in all our afflictions with his divine comfort, thus enabling us to comfort others with the comfort with which we ourselves have been comforted by God.

If the comfort offered in effective secular psychotherapy should be ultimately and hiddenly the comfort of God by which we ourselves are comforted, this need not mean that we must articulate this in an overt, verbal message of comfort, although it may indeed be mediated through words. It means rather that we consciously participate in the healing reality of the accepting love of God and mediate to others that reality which we ourselves have received. If from time to time this grace cries out to be articulated, it most of all asks to be inconspicuously mediated through concrete empathetic relationships.

As " the kingdom of God does not consist in talk but in power " (I Cor. 4:20), likewise psychotherapy does not consist merely in talk, but in the power mediated through this unique personal relationship, which finally consists in making transparent the power of the accepting reality present in life itself. Talking is merely functional to that more essential process of making unconditional acceptance transparent. Paul writes to the church at Corinth in the same spirit: "When I came to you, brethren, I did not come proclaiming to you the testimony of God in lofty words or wisdom. . . . I was with you in weakness and in much fear and trembling; and my speech and my message were not in plausible words of wisdom, but in demonstration of the Spirit and power, that your faith might not rest in the wisdom of men but in the power of God" (I Cor. 2:1-5). The authentic proclamation of the kerygma involves the demonstration of the power of God's acceptance, binding up the demonic powers and embodying forgiving love in concrete interpersonal relationships.

4. The Quest for Christ in Psychotherapy

Our remaining task is to set forth and defend the following special thesis: *All psychotherapy embodies an expectation for deliverance analogous to the Christ hopes of the Judeo-Christian tradition.* Four statements must be clarified if we are to show how the quest for the Christ is an extricable ingredient of all psychotherapy: (*a*) The expectation of deliverance from human bondage is a component of all psychotherapy; (*b*) Christ means Expected Deliverer; (*c*) the ministry of Jesus radically revolutionizes all human Christ expectations; and (*d*) the Christian community alleges that Jesus *is* the Christ.

Step one: *The expectation of deliverance from human bondage is a component of all modern psychotherapy.* People who come for help and commit themselves to this agonizing, time-consuming, and costly process of psychotherapy do so only on the basis of the fundamental expectation that somehow, through some miracle or technical device or medication or information, they might be delivered from the anxiety, guilt, and despair which blocks their full functioning. They come in the hope that something might be revealed which will illumine the meaning of their lives. They come with the expectation that the health (*salvus*) for which they have long yearned may now be within their grasp. Some such expectation is often the only motivation strong enough to cause them to forgo pretenses to normalcy, suffer the inner pain, and pay the stiff price which is often involved in modern psychotherapy. Furthermore, without such an expectation the propelling force of the therapeutic relationship would be severely reduced. The therapist can be of little help unless the individual is really experiencing anxiety, vulnerability, and is hurting enough to ask for help.

So the troubled person sets out on the long, difficult, often tedious, frightening, and agonizing journey of self-exploration, in the *hope* that somehow finally a great day will arrive when things will be different, when wholeness will be experienced rather than merely hoped for, when life will be uprighted, existence justified. On that day, partly mythological, partly realistic, he will be reconciled,

free to accept himself, be himself! Although there are infinite possible ways to symbolize this expectation, it must
be symbolized in some fashion, or the whole effort is a
waste of time. On that day he will be whole, alive, a fully
functioning person! Some new source of self-understanding will be revealed in terms of which he will be reassured
that his life is not a total failure, but that he is valued and
valuable, that he is " O.K." in the universe.[16]

This day of expectation might be called an eschatological hope, in the sense of a hoped-for *eschaton,* an end
time, final day of fulfillment of the promise of human
existence. In this sense, no therapy proceeds without some
eschatological hope. This hope may be variously symbolized as the day when I stop wheezing, the day when I no
longer feel afraid of everyone, the day I sell my millionth
dollar of life insurance, the day when the revolution suc-
ceeds, the day when I am given the keys to the executive's
bathroom, the day when I am loved by the girl I love, but
however it is symbolized, it is a necessary ingredient in
the chemistry of psychotherapeutic growth.

Actually, of course, *all men,* not just those in psychotherapy, share such expectations for self-fulfillment. All
lives are in some sense ultimately pointed toward some
eschatological vision. The desperate, urgent form of hope
that motivates effective psychotherapy is only a more
dramatic portrayal of the hope which all men in some
sense share, cast in the bold relief of crippled psychic functioning. Often the client in psychotherapy appears something like the hardened revolutionary who, perhaps against
great odds, is struggling valiantly against an old tyrannical
regime (himself, his old neurotic self-understanding), in
the fervent hope that a new regime is dawning. He *must*
maintain that commitment to that hope, else his whole
risky revolutionary fight would be quite impossible. Some

such expectation is an indispensable element of the revolution that we call effective psychotherapy.

Step two: *Christ means Expected Deliverer*. This longing for fulfillment dramatized particularly in psychotherapy but shared by all men took a particular shape in the history of the people of Israel as their historic expectation of *the Messiah*, an Expected Deliverer, the Anointed One who was to come amid cataclysmic events at the end of history to fulfill the promises of Israel, to deliver the people from bondage, and to inaugurate the reign of God. The Greek word that translated this hoped-for deliverer, the Messiah, was: *Christos*, the Christ. There is therefore a profound sense in which all persons seriously engaged in psychotherapy are *expecting the Christ*, if Christ is understood in the sense of a delivering event which will bring human existence to fulfillment and wholeness.

The kinds of longings that are everywhere evident in serious psychotherapy (the longing for comfort and renewal, the longing for release from guilt, the longing for wholeness and fulfillment, the longing for freedom from depressive moods) are not substantially different from the special longing of the people of Israel in their historic hope for a mighty deliverer who would upright history, initiate the Kingdom of God, and fulfill the promises of God to the people of Israel. Thus, living toward the Christ is a universally human phenomenon, not merely known to the people of Israel, but an inevitable component of human existence, and yet one that is focused with special urgency in the drama of psychotherapy. In this sense, *the expected Christ is therefore the reality which every man knows most deeply insofar as he knows himself*.

If meaning is essentially *yet* to be revealed, however, and if fulfillment is still in the future tense, if the Christ is still *awaited*, then it tends to make the *now* a time of

emptiness. *Now* we are caught in the seemingly endless
struggle with these guilts, anxieties, and compulsions
which ancient man called demonic powers. But on *that
day* things will be different. *Then* we will know ourselves
as known, valued, loved, reconciled, received, into the
bosom of creation itself. Now we experience life as relatively meaningless (relative, that is, to the future event of
meaning yet to be disclosed). The young lover awaits his
beloved, the student awaits graduation, the executive
awaits a skyrocketing sales report, the baseball club awaits
the day it will have another crack at the pennant. But
now is a time of boredom, of waiting for meaning to be
revealed. *Then* it will be different. Life then can be lived!
We will be resurrected from this now-death.

Step three: *The ministry of Jesus of Nazareth initiated a
radical revolution in the character of all human Christ
expectations.*[17] It was into just such a context of expectation that there appeared on the scene of history a man
named Jesus of Nazareth. A Jew, he came at a time when
the fervent expectation of Israel was at its most intense
pitch. For there were many who went flocking to the
desert, literally, to await the coming of the end of days,
the *eschaton,* the time of final judgment and fulfillment!
Pious communities dotted the edge of the Dead Sea composed of those who had fled all worldly values in order to
do nothing but *await* the coming of that expected event
when the sickness of history would be ended and the new
era of the reign of God would begin! The Anointed One
of God himself was expected to appear from the clouds
and establish his rightful and just rule over history. Such
was the context into which the man Jesus of Nazareth appeared.

Although we know little about this man except that
which has been reported about him by people whose lives,

according to their own witness, have been totally revolutionized by him (and so from them we can hardly expect an " objective " report), this much at least is clear: it was in response to the ministry of this man that a community arose which came to affirm something radically new about the character of all human expectations. For them the question of their life expectations, and in fact all human Christ hopes, had to be radically revised in their encounter with this man.

Whatever one may think about the strange and remarkable claims made concerning this man, at least this much is undeniable, that a community arose in response to him which has understood that all its Christ expectations are totally challenged and transformed by him. The style of his life and the events surrounding his death were such as to cause many who encountered him to remember him as one who was indeed the very source of health, the sign of the end time, the inaugurator of the reign of God, the authentic self-disclosure of the accepting reality at the heart of life itself!

His message was direct and simple: *The expected deliverance for which you yearn is at hand!* (Mark 1:15). The saving event toward which your life has been directed is presently revealed! (Matt. 10:7; Luke 22:18.) The reign of God is not to be awaited, but is *now*, and now to be received (Luke 11:20). The time of fulfillment is not a yet-to-be, but *now!* (Matt. 6:10; Luke 11:2.)

He announced good news: God is with us! God is for us! (Luke 4:16-18). The Kingdom of Heaven is now in the midst of you (Luke 10:9, 11). He confronted everyone he met with the simple either/or decision: receive and enter the Kingdom which is now coming into being, rejoice and live in it, *or* live under the tyranny of the old age already hastening toward destruction (Mark 12:34).

He spoke of himself modestly as the Sign of Jonah (Luke 11:30), the one who merely points to the dawning of the judgment and grace of God. When identified by Peter as the Christ, "he charged and commanded . . . [his disciples] to tell this to no one" (Luke 9:21). When asked by the high priest at his trial for blasphemy, "Are you the Christ?" Jesus is remembered as answering merely, "You have said so" (Matt. 26:64; cf. Luke 22:70-71), and he refused to answer further charges against him (Matt. 27:14; Mark 15:5).

To guilty men he announced: "Your sins are forgiven!" (Luke 7:48). The one who values you amid your value negations is fully present in history *now*. To anxious men he said: Be not anxious, for the One who cares for you ultimately is *now* in your midst, and making himself known in these last days as trustworthy (Matt. 6: 25-34). To men whose lives were organized around various illusory Christ hopes, he announced this paradoxically good (yet bad) news: the inner meaning of your expectation is *already* at hand. If you understand it properly, if you read the signs of the times properly, you will know that the deepest fulfillment for which you yearn is now already at hand, although it may not be in the form you had expected (Matt. 16:1-4).

Understandably his good news was interpreted as bad news to those who had their hopes fastened on more attractive Christ expectations than this now-moment which he offered. Understandably, he was regarded as a threat, inasmuch as he did not honor the fanciful, illusory Christ hopes which tend to characterize common human existence. And understandably he was so threatening to those who guided the religious and political structures for which his message was so upsetting that he himself was in danger and finally was crucified.

Step four: *Is Jesus the Christ?* One would think that a crucifixion would do away with a petty insurrectionist. Strangely enough, his very death made it necessary to focus anew the basic question which Jesus' life itself had framed: Is the Christ at hand? Is the expected end-time event already *now?*

The events that surrounded Jesus' death actually became the source of the greatest disturbance, which shook to the core the Christ hopes of the remembering community which followed him. Whatever was remembered about this man was remembered in the mirror of the events which clustered around his death. For this Rabbi, the bearer of the good news that life is now to be lived amid the living reality of the reign of God, affirmed death in the same way that he had affirmed life (Mark 14:32-42). When death came as the consequence of a life authentically lived, then death itself was to be received joyfully as God's own gift (Mark 8:27-37; Luke 23:46).

In addition to all these strange events, however, the strangest of all was yet to come. It sounds almost ridiculous to relate it. It is embarrassing to modern men. We would slightly prefer to leave this part of the story untold, since it is too fantastic for us. But it must be told: He is remembered as one who rose from the dead! (Matt., ch. 28; Mark, ch. 16; Luke, ch. 24).

It serves little purpose to try to argue on the grounds of objective history that his resurrection was a demonstrable fact. Faith is not a response to historical argumentation. But this much again is clear beyond doubt: A community of faith arose in response to the events of his last days which witnessed to his living presence in their midst as signifying the final Word of God, the radical affirmation by God of his Messianic vocation (Acts 2:36-39; 17:3).

In response to this, faithful Jews who had earnestly

longed for the end-time deliverance oddly enough began to raise the question of *the Messiah* in connection with this man! The beginning of the Christian community can be summarized in one simple question: *Is Jesus the Christ?* (John 4:29; Acts 2:36). They began to put the astonishing question which is still a question for decision for every man with Christ expectations: Could Jesus himself be the Expected Deliverer? Is the end time already *at hand?* Is he himself the sign of the end time? Could he embody the *end* of all our Christ expectations?

What an outrageous scandal the question itself was to many who had more exalted conceptions of the Messianic figure. Surely the Expected Deliverer would not be a Sabbath breaker, who sat with sinners and tax collectors, talked with prostitutes, offended religious authorities, and died on a cross! Not him.

If this question was an offense to traditional religious expectations, it remains a scandal and an offense to our modern, secularized, humanistic expectations. For any modern man who is still awaiting meaning to be revealed in his life is in a sense still waiting for the Christ. It is a haunting query which today confronts our secular mind with just as basic a decision about our Christ hopes as it did when originally framed in the context of Jewish apocalyptic hopes: Is Jesus the Christ? It remains a question for decision in every context, not the least of which is the psychotherapeutic relationship.

To affirm that Jesus is the Christ is to affirm that the reality which we meet in the *now* is the reconciling, forgiving, renewing reality which is proclaimed and celebrated in the therapeutic ministry of Jesus of Nazareth. Thus if psychotherapy exists in quest for the Christ, the *kerygma* announces the end of all our Christ quests.

NOTES

Preface

1. If this discussion seems to neglect or ignore certain live options and significant writings in the recent dialogue between theology and psychology, such as those of Mowrer, Tournier, Fromm, and Williams, then it should be indicated that a more thorough dialogical discussion is projected for the sequel to this volume, which was originally planned to be included in this discussion. If this volume essentially sets forth our constructive thesis, the second volume will attempt to clarify the relation of this proposal to other significant alternatives. The three principal contributions with which we understand ourselves to be in dialogical tension are those of Paul Tillich (as representative of a dehistorized ontology, as opposed to a covenant ontology), Eduard Thurneysen (as a chief representative of a type of pastoral care that reduces counseling to proclamation), and Seward Hiltner (as leading spokesman for a creative generation of American Protestantism that has tended to approach the situation of pastoral care with a diluted and functional Christology). In each of these cases we will spell out a more detailed appreciation and critique of these views than can be done here.

2. Quoted from a letter from Carl Rogers written July 9, 1965, in response to Chapter III. In earlier correspondence he commented on the argument of Chapters I and II as follows: "I think that you seem to grasp the essential principles of my own point of view. . . . Perhaps it is because of the summer I spent in Japan some time ago that I find myself slightly offended by the calm assumption that the Christian religion and the Christian view is the all-important thing. In Japan, of course, I found people interested in translating my views into a Buddhist frame of reference, which seems an equally valid

process to me. . . . Perhaps more importantly, I do agree with you that the counselor assumes ' that it is written into the universe that the individual *is* acceptable.' I think some counselors do not recognize this, and it is a good thing to have it pointed out."

CHAPTER I

THE IMPLICIT ASSUMPTION OF EFFECTIVE PSYCHOTHERAPY

1. Paul Tillich, " Theology and Counseling," *Journal of Pastoral Care* (Hereafter *JPC*), Winter, 1956; *The Courage to Be,* Ch. 2 (Yale University Press, 1952); Knox Kreutzer, " Approaches to a Theology of Psychotherapeutic Experience," *JPC*, Winter, 1959; R. L. Hudson, " Sin and Sickness," *JPC*, Summer, 1956; Daniel Day Williams, *The Minister and the Care of Souls* (Harper & Row, Publishers, Inc., 1961), pp. 11–30, 71 ff., 122 ff.; E. N. Ducker, *Psychotherapy: A Christian Approach* (London: George Allen & Unwin, Ltd., 1964), pp. 108 ff.

2. Thomas Hora, " Psychotherapy, Existence and Religion," *Psychoanalysis and Existential Philosophy* (E. P. Dutton & Company, Inc., 1962), pp. 70–80; Rollo May, "Toward the Ontological Basis of Psychotherapy," *Existential Inquiries,* Vol. 1, No. 1 (Sept., 1959).

3. Karl Barth, *Church Dogmatics,* Vol. II, Part One, *The Doctrine of God* (Edinburgh: T. & T. Clark, 1936), pp. 63–256. (Hereafter *CD.*) Quotations are used by permission of T. & T. Clark, 38 George Street, Edinburgh 2, Scotland.

4. *Psychoanalysis* is a type of psychotherapy that is informed by the analytical categories and diagnostic approach of Sigmund Freud. *Client-centered therapy* is a type of psychotherapy emerging out of the tradition of Rank, Taft, and Rogers, which rejects diagnosis and emphasizes reliance upon the resources for self-direction available within the client.

5. Carl Rogers, *Client-centered Therapy* (Houghton Mifflin Company, 1951), Part I. (Hereafter *CCT.*) Quotations are used by permission of the publisher.

6. Karl Barth, *CD,* Vol. IV, *passim.*

7. In "Pastoral Counseling and Traditional Theology," *Scottish Journal of Theology,* Donald Evans argues that, contrary to the typical psychotherapeutic deprecation of the role of religion, traditional Christian theology is capable of producing therapeutic insight and mature personality change. Although he proposes that " non-directive counseling " (as he persists in

calling it) is not inconsistent with "traditional theology" (the content of which is not spelled out) but that certain dangers must be avoided in their *rapprochement*, he fails to clarify in any more than general terms what these pitfalls are.

8. I suspect that the situation I have described, in which I have found myself compelled to relate to the student in terms of two seemingly conflicting offices (teacher and counselor), is not essentially different from the potential role conflict of the pastor, who is called to relate to his parishioner both as proclaimer of the Word and as helper-counselor. Undoubtedly it would be easier if he were just a preacher or just a counselor, but he is in fact both and cannot responsibly evade either task. Similarly, if I do a responsible job of teaching theology, I am called to take a position over against my hearer as self-consistently as possible, and from time to time it will be necessary to destroy weak and idolatrous foundations and apply the scalpel to cancerous assumptions that would ultimately prove harmful to the church's mission. Then I find myself counseling the same student to whom I teach theology. Counseling is not teaching, much less proclamation. The liberating word that comes to him must come from himself and not from me. I am perfectly clear about this in my own mind, if unclear about many other things, that the task of counseling must not be confused either with teaching or preaching. But how do these ostensibly conflicting offices interrelate and illuminate each other so that both can be self-consistently internalized and embodied in a single ministry? This is our question and task.

9. The excellent discussion by Robert Bonthius, "What Is Christian Counseling?" *JPC*, Summer, 1959, pp. 69–79, raises the question of whether Christian pastoral counseling is different from secular psychotherapy.

10. Cf. Fred Paddock, "A Philosophical Investigation of the Relation Between Psychoanalysis and Theology," *JPC*, Spring, 1959, pp. 38–42.

11. Rogers, *CCT*, pp. 22 ff.

12. Tillich, in *The Courage to Be* (p. 165), states this point succinctly: "The healer, in this relationship, does not stand for himself as an individual but represents the objective power of acceptance and self-affirmation."

13. Luke 15:11-24; Romans 3:21 ff.; Eph. 2:1-10.

14. John 1:14-16; Acts 2:22 ff.; Heb. 1:1-5.

15. Paul Tillich, *The Shaking of the Foundations* (Charles Scribner's Sons, 1948), pp. 153–164.

16. Rudolf Bultmann, *Der Begriff der Offenbarung im Neuen*

Testament (Tübingen: J. C. B. Mohr, 1929), pp. 1 ff.; Gustaf Aulén, *The Faith of the Christian Church* (Muhlenberg Press, 1948), pp. 22–79.

17. Aulén, *op. cit.*, pp. 14–16.

18. "God and faith hold close together," according to Luther (*Larger Catechism*), and to speak of one demands speech about the other. Faith is grounded in revelation, and revelation is perceived by the eye of faith. Since faith has the character of *response* to something that has gone before it, there is an ontological and logical priority of revelation to faith. In another (secondary) sense, however, there is a psychological and epistemological priority of the knower to the known, the believer to the object of devotion, and therefore a priority of faith to revelation.

19. Albert Outler, ed., *John Wesley* (Oxford University Press, Inc., 1964), *passim;* Colin W. Williams, *John Wesley's Theology Today* (Abingdon Press, 1960), pp. 23–39.

20. H. R. Niebuhr, *The Meaning of Revelation* (The Macmillan Company, 1952), pp. 138 ff.; *A Handbook of Christian Theology*, ed. by M. Halverson (Meridian Books, Inc., 1958), pp. 327–329; Rudolf Bultmann, *Existence and Faith* (Meridian Books, Inc., 1960), pp. 58–92.

21. *CCT*, Part I.

22. Existential psychology and psychotherapy are an exception.

23. Psychotherapy expresses a more radical understanding of the human predicament, however, than does the Socratic method, since compulsive syndromes constantly abort the birth process.

24. R. W. Heine, *A Comparison of Patients' Reports on Psychotherapeutic Experience with Psychoanalytic, Non-directive and Adlerian Therapists* (University of Chicago doctoral dissertation, 1950).

25. University of Chicago dissertation, 1949.

26. *Journal of Consulting Psychology*, 1950, Vol. 14, pp. 239–245.

27. Cf. also Fiedler's "Quantitative Studies on the Role of Therapists' Feelings Toward Their Patients," in O. H. Mowrer, ed., *Psychotherapy: Theory and Research* (The Ronald Press Company, 1953).

28. Sidney M. Jourard, *The Transparent Self: Self-disclosure and Well-Being* (D. Van Nostrand Company, Inc., 1964), p. 62. (Hereafter *TS.*)

29. Sigmund Freud, *Therapy and Technique* (Collier Books, 1963), p. 147.

30. *Ibid.*, p. 59.

31. *Ibid.*, p. 57.

32. *Ibid.*, p. 124.

33. *Ibid.*, pp. 123–124.

34. *Ibid.*, p. 122.

35. Sidney M. Jourard, "Self-disclosure and Other-Cathexis," *Journal of Abnormal and Social Psychology*, 1959, Vol. 59, pp. 428–431; "Self-disclosure Patterns in British and American College Females," *Journal of Social Psychology*, 1961 (c), Vol. 54, pp. 315–320; S. M. Jourard and P. Lasakow, "Some Factors in Self-disclosure," *J. Abnorm. Soc. Psychol.*, 1958, Vol. 56, pp. 91–98. Cf. also Jourard, *Personal Adjustment: An Approach Through the Study of Healthy Personality* (The Macmillan Company, 1958).

36. *TS*, p. 11.

37. *TS*, p. 21.

38. *TS*, p. 5.

39. *TS*, p. 11.

40. Maslow, Goldstein, Moustakas, Rogers, and others have anticipated many of Jourard's conclusions, but without employment of self-disclosure as a central construct.

41. *TS*, p. 5.

42. *TS*, p. 9.

43. *TS*, p. 64.

44. *TS*, Preface, iv.

45. *TS*, p. 154.

46. *TS*, p. 4.

47. *TS*, p. 30.

48. *TS*, p. 153.

Chapter II

THE EXPLICIT PROCLAMATION OF THE KERYGMA

1. Karl Barth, *CD*, II/1, pp. 79 ff.

2. *Ibid.*, p. 229.

3. André Godin, S.J., "Revelation and Psychotherapy II," *Continuum*, Winter, 1965, a critical response to Thomas C. Oden, "Revelation in Psychotherapy I," *Continuum*, Summer, 1964.

4. David A. Stewart, *Preface to Empathy* (Philosophical Library, Inc., 1956), pp. 12 ff.

5. Philip Schaff and Henry Wace, eds., *Nicene and Post-Nicene Fathers*, Vol. XIV, *The Seven Ecumenical Councils* (Wm. B. Eerdmans Publishing Company, 1956), pp. 243–297. (Hereafter Schaff.) Cf. Barth, *CD*, I/1, pp. 457 ff.

6. Robert L. Katz, *Empathy: Its Nature and Uses* (London: Collier-Macmillan, Ltd., 1963), p. 157.

7. Luke 2:1-20; 22:39-46; John 15:1-11; Rom. 5:6-8; 6:1-11.

8. Buber's distinction between I-Thou and I-It relationships parallels this point. Although Buber has rejected the term empathy as an adequate construct to describe authentic interpersonal dialogue, nonetheless when he speaks of "experiencing the other side," or "concrete imagining," his language refers to the same process we have attempted to describe.

9. Repeatedly the Old Testament prophets, psalms, and wisdom literature bear witness to the unsearchable, immeasurable understanding of God and conceive of human understanding under the analogy of God's understanding of man: "Happy is the man who finds wisdom, and the man who gets understanding. . . . The Lord by wisdom founded the earth; by understanding he established the heavens" (Prov. 3:13, 19). Cf. also Job 11:6; 28:20-23; Ps. 119; 136:5; 147:5; Isa. 40:28; Jer. 10:12; 51:15.

10. Schaff, *op. cit.*, XIV, pp. 262-265, on the true humanity of the God-man.

11. Schaff, *op. cit.*, pp. 3 ff.

12. Carl R. Rogers, "A Theory of Therapy, Personality, and Interpersonal Relationships, as Developed in the Client-centered Framework," in *Psychology: A Study of a Science*, ed. by Sigmund Koch (McGraw-Hill Book Company, Inc., 1959), p. 206. (Hereafter *PSS*.)

13. *PSS*, pp. 213 ff.

14. Katz, *op. cit.*, p. 44.

15. Theodor Reik, *Listening with the Third Ear* (Farrar, Straus and Giroux, Inc., 1949), p. 468.

16. Katz, *op. cit.*, pp. 38-39.

17. *PSS*, p. 210.

18. Schaff, *op. cit.*, p. 264.

19. *Ibid.*, p. 217.

20. *Ibid.*, p. 346.

21. Paul Tillich, *Systematic Theology*, Vol. II (The University of Chicago Press, 1957), pp. 97 ff.

22. Tillich's discussion of an ontology of anxiety, *The Courage to Be*, pp. 32 ff., and the courage to accept acceptance, pp. 155 ff., stands in the background of this subsection, although Tillich rejects the procedure of *analogia fidei*.

23. Rom. 5:6-11; Eph. 2:4-16; I John 4:10.

24. For a careful discussion of grace as permission, see Barth, *CD*, II/2, section 37, and III/4, pp. 49 ff.

25. For an empirical study showing the importance of acceptance in psychotherapy, see James E. Dittes, "Galvanic Skin Response as a Measure of Patient's Reaction to Therapist's Permissiveness," *J. Abnorm. Soc. Psychol.*, 1957, Vol. 55, pp. 295–303.

26. Carl Rogers, *On Becoming a Person* (Houghton Mifflin Company, 1961), p. 17. (Hereafter *OBP*.) Quotations are used by permission of the publisher.

27. Karen Horney, *Neurosis and Human Growth* (W. W. Norton & Company, Inc., 1950), pp. 176 ff.

28. Rogers, *CCT*, pp. 22–23, pp. 35–41.

29. Rom. 6:1-11; 12:1-21; Col. 1:21 to 3:17. Cf. Barth, *CD*, III/4; Thomas C. Oden, *Radical Obedience* (The Westminster Press, 1964), pp. 95 ff.; Carl Rogers, *OBP*, pp. 163 ff.

30. Rudolf Bultmann, *Kerygma and Myth*, ed. H. W. Bartsch (London: S.P.C.K., 1957), pp. 26–31.

31. *OBP*, p. 283.

32. John 17:18; I Cor., ch. 13; II Cor. 5:19; Eph. 3:14-19; I John 4:7-10. Cf. Erich Fromm, *The Art of Loving* (Harper & Row, Publishers, Inc., 1956), pp. 7 ff.; Søren Kierkegaard, *Works of Love* (Harper & Row, Publishers, Inc., 1962), *passim;* Carl Rogers, *OBP*, pp. 163–199.

33. Emil Brunner, *The Divine Imperative* (The Westminster Press, 1947), pp. 53 ff.; Paul Lehmann, *Ethics in a Christian Context* (Harper & Row Publishers, Inc., 1963), pp. 23 ff., 124 ff.

34. Our argument that human care is properly viewed under the analogy of God's care for us is anticipated by John Deschner, who writes in *The Student World* (First Quarter, 1954, pp. 1 ff.): "In pastoral care, we deal not with good counsel, but with the good Lord who is on the side of the one in need, fighting his battle for him. It is *news* because it tells not just of good advice, but of a change in the situation itself. It is *good* news, because it tells, not just of new resources, but that the master of the situation has now arrived on our side." We must begin our pastoral care "not simply from the desire to help each other. We begin with the one who has really brought help." Pastoral care points us, first of all, to the "true pastor — the shepherd — and with him pastoral care begins and ends." "*Pastoral care becomes serious when we see it in the light of the pastoral care of God for us.*" It is not only the skilled expert psychotherapist who has a therapeutic task, but in the light of the priesthood of all believers, it becomes a question of how each one of us takes care of the other, how every man

is a neighbor to the other. God's pastoral care for us causes us to redefine human need, and ask " if the need we see is the need that actually exists, the need that God sees." We may use, but not ultimately trust, our analyses of human need. It is in the revelation of God in Jesus Christ that our understanding of human need is finally illumined. Cf. André Dumas, " The Biblical Foundation of Spiritual Help," *Student World*, First Quarter, 1954.

CHAPTER III

THE THEOLOGY OF CARL ROGERS

1. For a fuller account of this triadic structure for systematic theology, see Thomas C. Oden, *The Community of Celebration* (National Methodist Student Movement, 1964), pp. 127–140, where this threefold sequence is related to worship, the Christian year, and preaching, as well as psychotherapy.

2. In Koch, ed., *PSS*.

3. " Toward a Modern Approach to Values: The Valuing Process in the Mature Person," *J. Abnorm. Soc. Psychol.*, Vol. 68, Feb., 1964, pp. 160 ff. (Hereafter *MAV*.)

4. *OBP*, pp. 125–162.

5. *OBP*, p. 8.

6. *PSS*, p. 186.

7. *PSS*, p. 192 (italics mine).

8. *PSS*, p. 193.

9. *PSS*, p. 191.

10. *PSS*, p. 191.

11. *PSS*, p. 187.

12. *PSS*, p. 192.

13. *OBP*, p. 26.

14. *OBP*, p. 26.

15. Rom. 1:18 to 3:20; Augustine, " On Free Will " (*De libero arbitrio*), in The Library of Christian Classics, Vol. VI, *Augustine: Earlier Writings* (London: SCM Press, Ltd., 1953), pp. 102–218; Calvin, *Institutes of the Christian Religion* (London: T. & T. Clark, 1953), Book II, pp. 209 ff.

16. *MAV*, p. 161.

17. *PSS*, p. 196; cf. A. Maslow, *Toward a Psychology of Being* (D. Van Nostrand Company, Inc., 1962), pp. 3–19.

18. *MAV, loc. cit.*, p. 162.

19. " A Process Conception of Psychotherapy," *op. cit.*, pp. 132–133.

20. *PSS*, p. 203.

21. *PSS*, p. 200.
22. *PSS*, p. 197.
23. *PSS*, p. 203.
24. Calvin, *op. cit.*, Book II, Chs. 1–5; Søren Kierkegaard, *Fear and Trembling and The Sickness Unto Death* (Double-day & Company, Inc., 1955), pp. 146–156; cf. Bultmann, " The New Testament and Mythology," *Kerygma and Myth,* p. 31.
25. *PSS*, p. 205.
26. *PSS*, p. 210.
27. *PSS*, p. 209.
28. *OBP*, p. 27.
29. *PSS*, p. 204.
30. William Barclay, *A New Testament Wordbook* (Harper & Row, Publishers, Inc., n.d.), pp. 48–54.
31. Rogers, *PSS*, p. 213; *OBP*, pp. 61–62.
32. *OBP*, pp. 66–67.
33. *OBP*, pp. 50 ff.
34. *OBP*, p. 62.
35. *OBP*, p. 62; cf. *CCT*, pp. 24–33.
36. *PSS*, p. 208.
37. *PSS*, p. 207.
38. *PSS*, p. 213.
39. *OBP*, p. 35.
40. *OBP*, p. 33.
41. *OBP*, p. 55.
42. *CCT*, pp. 4–7.
43. *OBP*, pp. 39–59, 297–314, 338–347.
44. *OBP*, p. 5.
45. To be pursued in the sequel to this volume.
46. *PSS*, p. 216.
47. *OBP*, p. 132.
48. *OBP*, pp. 133–136.
49. *OBP*, pp. 137–152.
50. Albert Outler, *op. cit.*, pp. 9–10 n.
51. *OBP*, pp. 163 ff.
52. *OBP*, p. 66.
53. *MAV*, p. 164.
54. *MAV*, p. 166.
55. *CCT*, pp. 22 ff., 41 ff.
56. *OBP*, Part VI; *PSS*, pp. 241 ff.
57. Karl Barth, " Gospel and Law," in *Community, State and Church* (Doubleday & Company, Inc., 1960), pp. 71–101; Emil Brunner, *op. cit.*, pp. 140–152; Thomas C. Oden, *op. cit.*, pp. 94–116.

Chapter IV

BARTH'S DOCTRINE OF ANALOGY

1. Derived from the Greek *ana* (in, according to) and *logos* (ratio, proportion), *analogia* is often rendered "in right relationship to," "in agreement with" (Arndt and Gingrich, *A Greek-English Lexicon of the New Testament and Other Early Christian Literature* [University of Chicago Press, 1957], p. 56). Cf. Charles Hartshorne's article on "Analogy" in *An Encyclopedia of Religion*, ed. by V. Ferm (Philosophical Library, Inc., 1945), pp. 19 f. (Hereafter *ER*.) The English term "analogy" refers to "a relation of likeness, *between* two things or *of* one thing *to* or *with* another, consisting in the resemblance not of the things themselves but of two or more attributes, circumstances or effects; thus, the *analogy* between sleep and death lies in the attendant cessation of activity and appearance of repose." (*Webster's New International Dictionary of the English Language*, 2d ed., unabridged [G. & C. Merriam Co., Publishers, 1942], p. 94.)

2. David E. Roberts, *Psychotherapy and a Christian View of Man* (Charles Scribner's Sons, 1950), p. 151.

3. Dietrich Bonhoeffer, *Wer ist und wer war Jesus Christus?* (Hamburg: Furche-Verlag, 1962); *Prisoner for God* (The Macmillan Company, 1957); Joseph L. Hromádka, *Theology Between Yesterday and Tomorrow* (The Westminster Press, 1957); William Stringfellow, *Free in Obedience* (The Seabury Press, Inc., 1964); Helmut Gollwitzer, *Die Christliche Gemeinde in der politischen Welt* (Tübingen: J. C. B. Mohr [Paul Siebeck], 1955); Heinrich Ott, "What Is Systematic Theology?" in *The Later Heidegger and Theology*, ed. by Robinson and Cobb (Harper & Row Publishers, Inc., 1963).

4. *CD*, I/1, p. 279.

5. *CD*, I/1, p. 280.

6. *CD*, I/1, p. 279. The term "analogy of faith" was widely used by older orthodox Protestant theology to refer to a "correspondence of the several parts of divine revelation in one consistent whole" (McClintock and Strong, *Cyclopedia of Biblical, Theological and Ecclesiastical Literature* [Harper, 1896], Vol. I, p. 213), or "the harmonious relations discovered or recognized among the revealed truths of religion" (*New "Standard" Dictionary of the English Language* [Funk and Wagnalls Company, 1962], p. 100). Under this hermeneutic principle, Scripture must be exegeted according to the analogy

of faith, i.e., " in conformity with the confession of the church "
(F. W. Grosheide in *Encyclopedia of Christianity*, 1964).

7. Barth, *CD*, I/1, p. 279.

8. *CD*, II/1, p. 229.

9. *CD*, I/1, p. 1, thesis of paragraph 1 of *CD*.

10. *CD*, I/1, p. 11.

11. *CD*, I/1, pp. 11–12.

12. *CD*, II/1, p. 223.

13. *CD*, II/1, p. 231.

14. *CD*, II/1, p. 227.

15. Commenting on Heb. 3:13, quoted by Barth, *CD*, I/1,
p. 274.

16. *CD*, III/4, p. 245.

17. *CD*, III/4, p. 245.

18. *CD*, III/4, p. 246.

19. *CD*, II/1, p. 230.

20. *Ibid.*

21. *CD*, II/1, p. 76.

22. *CD*, II/1, p. 77 (italics mine).

23. *CD*, II/1, p. 83.

24. *CD*, II/1, p. 85. " It is not, then, the case that by means
of a clarification of the meaning and understanding of our
words as such we can press forward to a provisional meaning
and understanding of their use in relation to God," Barth argues. " The provisional meaning and understanding to which
we can, of course, press forward by this kind of clarification is
the provisional meaning and understanding of our understanding of the world, and finally of our self-understanding as it
may actually come to pass in our encounter or supposed encounter with one of the gods of this world," II/1, p. 230.

25. *CD*, II/1, p. 227.

26. *CD*, II/1, p. 234.

27. *CD*, II/1, p. 235.

28. *CD*, I/1, p. 274 (italics mine).

29. Gerald Phelan, *St. Thomas and Analogy* (Marquette
University Press, 1941), p. 10.

30. *CD*, II/1, p. 225.

31. David Roberts, *op. cit.*, pp. 104–118; Seward Hiltner,
Preface to Pastoral Theology (Abingdon Press, 1958), pp.
91 ff., 113 f.; Tillich, *The Courage to Be*, pp. 32–77; *Systematic
Theology*, Vol. II, pp. 29–85; Reinhold Niebuhr, *The Nature
and Destiny of Man* (Charles Scribner's Sons, 1953), Vol. I,
pp. 33–53; Robert Elliott, " Sin and Neurosis," unpublished
University of Chicago doctoral dissertation; O. Hobart Mowrer,

The Crisis in Psychiatry and Religion (D. Van Nostrand Company, Inc., 1961), pp. 40–59, 81–155.

32. Daniel Day Williams, *op. cit.*, pp. 11 ff., 71 ff.; Tillich, "Theology and Counseling," *JPC;* "On Healing," *Pastoral Psychology,* June, 1955, pp. 25–28; "The Relation of Religion and Health," *Pastoral Psychology,* May, 1954; Hiltner, *op. cit.*, pp. 89 ff.; *The Christian Shepherd* (Abingdon Press, 1959), pp. 11–24; Dayton G. Van Deusen, *Redemptive Counseling* (John Knox Press, 1960), pp. 79–102, 169 ff.; William E. Hulme, *Counseling and Theology* (Muhlenberg Press, 1956), *passim;* Kreutzer, *op. cit.*, pp. 197–209.

33. For a more detailed bibliography, see Thomas C. Oden, "Revelation in Psychotherapy I," *Continuum,* Summer, 1964, 239 n., 262 n., and *passim.*

34. The *locus classicus* of a "divine Magna Carta in the matter of health," according to Barth, is Ex. 15:26, "I am the Lord that healeth thee," *CD,* III/4, p. 369. All historical healing of men and nations is seen as the circumference of this center (II Kings 20:1 ff.; Ps. 30:2 f.; 107:17 ff.; I Cor. 12:9).

35. *CD,* III/4, p. 649.

36. *CD,* III/4, pp. 651–652.

37. *CD,* III/4, p. 386; cf. Rogers, *OBP,* pp. 163 ff.

38. *CD,* III/4, p. 388.

39. *CD,* III/4, p. 387.

40. *CD,* II/1, p. 168.

41. *CD,* II/1, p. 232.

42. *CD,* II/1, pp. 172 ff. This Trojan horse is decisively confronted in the declaration of Barmen, 1934, in response to Nazi claims for new revelations to be placed alongside Jesus Christ. The same issue has occurred repeatedly in the church's confrontation with idealism, positivism, nationalism, and socialism, all of which have wanted to have their say in the church alongside revelation. Although more subtle, the issue is formally the same in much of our aborted dialogue with psychotherapy.

43. *CD,* II/1, p. 232.

44. Psychologist Sidney Jourard has similarly argued that we cannot understand another person until we have been met by him in a revealing event (*TS,* pp. 4–11). Knowledge of the neighbor, as of God, is a response to his revelation of himself.

45. *CD,* II/1, p. 221.

46. Numbers, ch. 22; cf. Ex. 4:10 ff., Moses' slowness of speech when confronted with the call of God, and Jeremiah's confession (Jer. 1:6 ff.): "Lord, I cannot speak; for I am a child." *CD,* II/1, p. 221.

47. *CD*, III/4, p. 74.

48. That Jesus Christ is the noetic basis of creation means that only " as we know what free and absolutely basic and controlling grace is . . . only then do we know . . . what creation is." *CD*, III/4, p. 39. Grace is thus the ontic basis of creation: " It is not, then, the case that God first determined Himself as Creator, then made man his Creature, and only then in a later development and decision elected man and instituted His covenant with Him. On the contrary, it is for the sake of this election and in relation to this institution that He created heaven and earth and man. He created the universe in Jesus Christ," III/4, p. 39.

49. In his polemic against natural theology, however, Barth sometimes damages his own case by exaggeration. Protestant theology, he says, " has good reason to regard as quite uninteresting the man for whom natural theology can always be interesting," *CD*, II/1, p. 168. Barth's cause would have been better served if he had clarified what seems to be his deeper intention, that natural man apart from God is merely an abstraction, rather than " uninteresting," since the latter seems to imply that Christian faith can justifiably ignore the man who imagines himself to live without God, an implication Barth elsewhere denies (cf. IV/3 on mission). We would merely wish Barth to press his own doctrine of creation more consistently and take with all seriousness the idolatrous, natural man whom God himself has taken so seriously in Jesus Christ. Barth much too broadly calls for " a christological understanding of man on the basis of which his self-understanding must be ignored as *triviality*" (II/1, p. 171, italics mine). If he means that humanity can never be adequately understood by attending only to man's own limited estranged self-understanding allegedly apart from grace, we agree, but if he means that authentic faith is utterly disinterested in all natural self-understanding then that is inconsistent with his doctrine of the covenant as the clue to creation.

50. *CD*, II/1, p. 81.

51. Phelan, *op. cit.*, p. 23.

52. Thomas Aquinas wrote, " We can speak of the creature resembling God in some way, but not of God resembling the creature," *Summa Theologica*, Ia, iv.3, 4, quoted in Thomas Gilby, ed., *St. Thomas Aquinas: Theological Texts* (London: Oxford University Press, 1955), p. 8.

53. James D. Collins, *God in Modern Philosophy* (Henry Regnery Company, 1959), p. 399.

54. *Ibid.*, p. 3.

55. *De Docta Ignorantia*, 1440.

56. Rudolf Bultmann, *Essays Philosophical and Theological* (The Macmillan Company, 1955), pp. 90 ff.; cf. Oden, *Radical Obedience*, chapter II.

57. Gottlieb Söhngen, "*Analogia Fidei*," *Catholica*, Heft 3, 4, 1934 (cf. Barth, *CD*, II/1, p. 82); Söhngen, "Wesen und Akt in der scholastischen Lehre von der participatio und analogia entis," *Stud. Gen.*, Heft 8, 1955, pp. 649–662; cf. W. Pannenberg, "Zur Bedeutung des Anal. Gedankens bei Karl Barth," *Theologische Literaturzeitung*, 78, 1953, pp. 17–24.

58. *CD*, II/1, p. 92. Cf. Barth, *Anselm: Fides Quaerens Intellectum* (The World Publishing Company, 1962), Intro.

59. Kegley and Bretall, eds., *The Theology of Paul Tillich* (The Macmillan Company, 1952), p. 179; "Tillich's Doctrine of God," pp. 164–198.

60. Charles Hartshorne, "Analogy," *ER*, p. 19. Cf. Hartshorne, *Man's Vision of God* (Archon Books, 1964), "The Theological Analogies and the Cosmic Organism," pp. 174–212.

61. Hartshorne, *ER*, p. 19. Cf. *Reality as Social Process* (The Free Press of Glencoe, 1953), pp. 110 ff.

62. *ER*, p. 20 (italics mine).

63. *ER*, p. 20 (italics mine); cf. *Man's Vision of God*, pp. 174 ff.

64. Hartshorne, *Reality as Social Process, passim.*

65. Rogers, *PSS*, pp. 200, 210.

66. Hartshorne, *Man's Vision of God*, p. 179; *ER*, 20; cf. *The Divine Relativity* (Yale University Press, 1948), pp. 116 ff.

67. Hartshorne, *ER*, p. 20; *Man's Vision of God*, pp. 177 ff.; Rogers, *CCT*, pp. 19 ff.

68. Söhngen, *op. cit.*; Hans U. von Balthasar, *Karl Barth: Darstellung und Deutung einer Theologie* (Cologne: J. Hegner, 1951); Hans Küng, *Justification* (Thomas Nelson & Sons, 1964).

69. *CD*, II/1, section 26.

70. *CD*, II/1, p. 88 (italics mine).

71. *CD*, II/1, p. 146.

72. *CD*, II/1, pp. 167 f.

73. *CD*, II/1, pp. 94, 95.

74. Barth, *How to Serve God in a Marxist Land*, with Johannes Hamel (Association Press, 1959), pp. 57–58.

75. *CD*, II/1, p. 93.

76. *CD*, III/4, p. 86.

77. *CD*, III/4, p. 496 (italics mine).

Chapter V

KERYGMA AND THERAPEIA

1. James Hope Moulton and George Milligan, *The Vocabulary of the Greek Testament*, Illustrated from the Papyri and Other Non-Literary Sources (Wm. B. Eerdmans Publishing Company, 1949), pp. 288, 289.

2. Arndt and Gingrich, *op. cit.*, p. 359.

3. Moulton and Milligan, *op. cit.*, p. 289; cf. Joseph Henry Thayer, ed., *A Greek-English Lexicon of the New Testament* (American Book Company, 1886), pp. 288–289.

4. Rudolf Bultmann, *Theology of the New Testament* (Charles Scribner's Sons, 1951), Vol. I, p. 205.

5. Arndt and Gingrich, *op. cit.*, p. 901.

6. Although *therapōn* never appears as a descriptive title for Jesus, its verb forms are constantly applied to his ministry, as may be verified in any good concordance.

7. The contemporary argument is formally the same, which proposes that psychic or somatic healing has no relationship with the saving purpose of God, whether the disjunction is proposed by secular or religious proponents.

8. Arndt and Gingrich, *op. cit.*, p. 432. Principal sources for examining the earliest forms of Christian kerygma are in Acts and the Pauline letters, the best summaries of which are found in Acts 2:14-39; 8:17-41; and I Cor. 15:1-7.

9. C. H. Dodd, *The Apostolic Preaching and Its Developments* (Harper & Row, Publishers, Inc., 1936), pp. 7 ff., 32 ff.

10. *Ibid.*, p. 7.

11. *Ibid.*, p. 8. Cf. Moulton and Milligan, *op. cit.*, p. 343.

12. Ernst Fuchs, *Studies of the Historical Jesus* (London: SCM Press, Ltd., 1964), pp. 11 ff., 213 ff.

13. Alfred Plummer, *A Critical and Exegetical Commentary on the Second Epistle of St. Paul to the Corinthians*, International Critical Commentary (Edinburgh: T. & T. Clark, 1951), pp. 6 ff.

14. Moulton and Milligan, *op. cit.*, p. 485.

15. Paul Minear, *The Kingdom and the Power* (The Westminster Press, 1950), pp. 137 ff.

16. Samuel Beckett's play *Waiting for Godot* is the most penetrating modern presentation of the Messianic expectation. In seeking to justify his expectation, Vladimir declares: "Yes, in this immense confusion one thing alone is clear. We are waiting for God to come. . . . We are not saints, but we have

kept our appointment. How many people can boast as much?"
to which Estragon replies: "Billions" (Grove Press, 1954),
p. 51.

17. Cf. Joseph W. Mathews, "The Christ of History," *Letter
to Laymen*, April, 1962.

3 5282 00727 2555